AKHENATEN SPEAKS

through the mediumship of

Maisie Besant

THE NATURE OF SPIRITUAL HEALING

ISBN 1 873545 01 0

Cover design by Jane Wisner.

Material compiled & edited by Greg Branson.

Published by The Eye of Gaza Press, BCM - New Age,
London, WC1N 3XX   (071 - 485 2304)

Printed by Carlyon Industries, 1c Carlyon Rd, Alperton,
Wembley, Middlesex. HA0 1HH   (081-998 0067)

CONTENTS

THE BEGINNING

In my development circle days, I was often given the description of a Chinese guide with me. Of the three gifts I would develop, teaching, clairvoyance and healing, he was for the healing.

I began work as a medium in December 1945. It was the following Summer that I was first asked to give healing. My doorbell unexpectedly rang and the lady standing on the doorstep told me she was trying to heal a spastic child and was not accomplishing it. Her guides had given my name as a healer who could help. I gladly responded, regularly visiting the child until an improvement came.

There were no other cases for a further six months. I had gone to take a service at a church in Southend. A healer friend accompanied me. Later she told me that during the service her guide had recommended that I visit a certain patient of hers. This man was a wartime casualty, and bits of schrapnel were embedded in his body that would sometimes work through to the surface causing him to suffer a great deal of pain. When I entered his room, he was sitting up in bed. He turned his head and said "I have been waiting for you." This took me by surprise, as my friend had not told him I was coming. While I gave healing, Ming, my chinese guide came through and spoke to him. I did not know at the time that he would only survive for a further six weeks.

The morning after, a telephone call from my friend informed me that this man had slept for twelve hours and woke free of pain for the first time in eighteen months. He continued without pain until the end.

I had been developing my mediumship for three years before I learnt that an Egyptian guide who had been speaking through me was in fact Akhenaten. A man who had made a study of the ancient Egyptian language came as a guest to my development circle. At the end of my usual trance talk he asked the speaker for his name. He replied Amenhotep IV, his name before he changed it to Akhenaten. The man then asked a question using the old Egyptian tongue. Akhenaten replied in the same language.

I subsequently learned that he was also known as "The Heretic Pharoah" because he upset the ecclesiastical authorities and worshipped the sun as the earthly appearance of the creator, replacing the many Egyptian gods which had become the focus of corruption by the priests. In concentrating on the one God of all life he foreshadowed the teaching of the Master Jesus. He transferred his seat of government to a new city built especially to celebrate this new religion. He also brought in a new form of art showing him not as a God but an ordinary king and family man. However the new initiative, opposed by his mother Oueen Tiye and his wife Nefertiti, could not be sustained and the very sensitive Akhenaten died eventually of a broken heart.

He has remained as my chief teaching guide to this day and oversees all the work done through me by my band of spirit helpers.

Maisie Besant

THE EYE OF GAZA

There is a powerful stream of divine creative power which links the ages and which finds expression in many times and many places but at its highest it was found in Egypt at Gizeh and after that in the Greece of Mount Olympus. To be "Eyeless in Gaza" is to turn away from the truths that are dispensed through the Gods to any seeker after spiritual progress.

As we move into this new age, the truths that were present in those early days need now to return to the earth upgraded and appropriate to these modern times, the creative archetypal forms that can find expression through the many souls now back in incarnation and banded together in encalves of power dedicated to this end. The creative aspects of the Godhead need new expression now to lift this harsh world onto a higher arc of experience, and the sword of justice needs to be returned to the earth.

The Eye of Gaza Press is committed to present some of the teachings that stem from these ancient times channeled through mediums and inspired writers that can strike a responsive chord in souls of today.

THE NATURE OF HEALING

It is with great pleasure that we come into this sanctuary to speak to you on the true nature of healing. Illness is attributed to so many things these days. Almost every week something new is discovered to be the cause of cancer, and while it is true these factors do accentuate the tendency to contract this disease, it is not so much what one takes into the body by way of nourishment that is responsible, but more the bitterness, hate and jealousy that many people hold to themselves, very often quite unconsciously, which are the real culprits. And when the floodgates within are released, these energies will get right through the etheric into the physical.

People who are sincerely treading a path of peace and prayer and service are not usually susceptible to these extremely destructive conditions, and it largely does not matter what is given to the body, provided they feel comfortable with it. The power of spiritual endeavour, even that which does not appear to be successful, can overcome much that would strike down a more materialistic person. So first we would say to you, don't be over-anxious about food. Look within for the real cause of any physical malfunctioning.

Man lives on three levels of being, primarily. There are other subdivisions which have their particular ramifications, but we want to concentrate on the major three, and these are the mind, the soul and the body.

The soul becomes dyed with man's thoughts, his words, his actions. As a man thinks, so surely he will become. The soul is the battleground where the spirit engages itself in warfare with the mind, which leads either to healing forces, the vitality of the spirit, becoming alive in the personality, or else to that deterioration when the whole sense life of the body has no active spark of spirit in it.

Except with some karmically induced states, or where a person has taken on an illness as a service to another soul, it should never happen that a physical condition is brought into being that cannot be dispersed and the knife has to be brought in. But where the mind is kept in too limited boundary, where it is not plastic enough, not receptive enough, not opening up to the enlightenment that could come, then no remedy or potion, no amount of laying on of hands, will reverse the condition.

Man is too comfort loving. He does not like facing what is there within his soul, and these bottled-up states that result are always breeding grounds for disease. Even the most integrated person must sometimes be willing to be jockeyed out of an easy time by some inner, hidden impulse and plunged into a period of chaos.

No new structure can be raised in the mind without the old, obsolete patterns first being removed. How often, when coming out of some distressing period in your life, have you said 'never again'? But seeking man must periodically face these times of testing and confusion, and they should be welcomed enthusiastically. To resist is to court disaster.

There is an analytical approach deep within the mind of man, as all who have entered into meditation know full well, that recognises motive as a ruling force. An artist may see a germ of something beautiful in what most people regard as ugly. When you look at yourselves in the mirror of spiritual reflection, you are sure to see the weaknesses, the soil that needs better nourishment coming in. But do you also see the beauty and the divine potential that is there?

You may sometimes feel that there is something within that is stopping you being able to communicate with your maker as you would like. And what do you do? Do you put aside the prayer and the meditation? Refuse to face this ugliness in yourself? Because if you do that you are leaving something important out of the reckoning. God reveals Himself through man's willingness to face the exposure of himself to himself.

There is a feeling within man who is beginning to know

himself, a fear of the loneliness he is going to meet, lest it should shrivel him up and make him unable to walk with certainty the path of earthly living that he must tread. But he must learn to overcome this fear, expand himself and be open to the rays of God's warmth and sunshine of spirit which are all around, but which he must place himself in the way of to receive. There are many things that a person seeking on the spiritual pathway will be forced to confront, and sometimes they are waiting in the corridors of his mind, like lurking thieves, ready to spring on him when he is least prepared.

There is a beautiful poem on your earth which starts off with the words 'Take time to be holy. Speak oft with thy Lord', and it goes on to expound about the quality that must arise within the soul before it can become a radiant, vital force that will reach out soul to soul. There's a new feeling abroad regarding soul communication, but not always expressed in the right way. Remember that everything that emanates from spirit can quickly be seized upon by the sense life, and a lot of unholy relationships and groupings of people can result.

When the soul does receive illumination this is really only an enlightened feeling that has come in and conquered the heart. The mind must then interpret this. Man does not leave his reason behind when he seeks to walk the spiritual pathway. And the higher the way of the mystic that man aspires to, so much more will his reasoning faculty be needed. But the intellect can trip the mind up. It can seize hold of it and make it its servant.

Have you ever stopped to think how intuition arises within you? There are times when you have a definite feeling that you may not be able to put into words, but you are aware that it is there growing within you, and leading you perhaps towards an encounter of the way, a meeting with some situation, some person, some group of people and when you enter into this your intuition takes you in its embrace. You know that here is something good, and perhaps for a while you are lifted up high on an emotional wavelength.

Oh, but how easy it is then to be lulled by the experience of entering into this pure love of God, or so it seems. There are many dreamers upon the earth, but there are not so many who can make their dreams a reality, not so many who are willing to pay the price of entry into a full living co-operation with this physical universe. The imaginative attitude has to come in and build on the feelings that are there with intelligently based thought-forms. Then gradually the canvas of the mind is going to be woven with colours, with structures that have got the true life in them. Spirit is ever forceful - never, never acquiescent. Something has got to be brought in to balance the emotion that can overpower the soul, and that something is the good sound reasoning faculty of the earth mind, which can focus and direct the energies into constructive activity.

As you know, you have an auric field around you. If you could tune into this reality that you truly are, you would be aware of the rays streaming out far beyond your body, some going down into the earth, some raying out from the heart centre, meeting, clashing sometimes, with those that come forward from other sources. And when these radiations are directed into a relationship, so you are going to get a soul identification with your brother man that will either heal or send in rays of destruction. Oh, how exacting are the responsibilities of high spiritual attainment.

If you could only see what happens when a person allows thoughts of malice, envy, greed to rise up and possess his soul. The thoughts that reflect the lower instinctual plane go out and link up with other thoughts of their kind. You would see them build up into large and ominous thought patterns into which the weak and misguided as well as the malevolent can tune and drawing these thoughts into themselves they magnify the discontent. Is this not what happened in Germany before the war, until there was no light strong enough to penetrate?

The thoughts that emanate from those who are becoming more spiritually inspired, they too build into great banks or clouds of thought energy. One exhibiting a dark, heavy, stormy process and the other sending out light,

4

airy rays of beauty and scintillation. You would see these two converge, and some of this heavy, stormy thought would simply fall flat - that is when the good thought patterns have the necessary strength and penetration. It is not always so.

Sometimes the stormy cloud sucks in greedily of the other, and then, triumphant, races to other parts of the globe where violence, hate and greed live. That cloud bank descends and forms around the peoples of the earth committing, or planning to commit, dire atrocities. And this will hold sway until such time as a greater cloud bank of the good and true can come in and make it fall to the earth.

When man is in the grip of negative thoughts, these collect around his body and stimulate the lower emotions. Have you not had some emotion take you completely in its grasp? Fear can render you completely impotent, and hatred seems as though a fire is raging away in your body. And what is the result if this is allowed to control the body? It is perhaps going to weaken the heart. The muscles will become flabby, the pumping action spasmodic and uncontrolled.

All these things at work on the lower sensual life of man have a depleting and deteriorating influence on the body. It's going to lose its elasticity. The mind, too, will become torpid and heavy. All this opens the way for disease.

Aspiring man must cultivate the good and strong thought patterns, must keep the mind fixed on higher things, and above all must be ready to go through the soul disciplines that become necessary, when it may indeed seem as though the heart is divided from the will.

This is an initiation pathway that no spiritual seeker can possibly hope to avoid. There are no short cuts. All must climb the steep, steep hill of determined effort. Man lives by effort, surely. And he must learn to reach out to others, through the astral body (so closely linked to the sense life), to become aware of a wonderful sense of companionship that will build up in those places where people meet regularly in prayer and good fellowship.

Something of spirit breathes in those places. Thought forms build up and are supplemented by other thought banks brought forward from past ages. And gradually the atmosphere becomes alive. An energy is created that heightens the perceptions, motivates development, and where the heart gravitates towards service, as it should do, the thought patterns are used time and time again to benefit those who reach out in need. Truly then, the laws of spirit are being fully utilised, and healing becomes a natural and ever-expanding process.

God bless you all.

THE BODIES OF MAN

It is with that very real concern for you who are seeking along spiritual pathways that we once again encourage your hearts and minds to follow after the rays of light we shall put before you, to help you understand your bodies a little better, and to give you clearer indications of how best to give and receive healing. For it is as much an art for the healer to be able to lift himself above those things of the earthly life that he may have brought with him to the place of healing as it is for the patient to be open and receptive.

So first we should like to say a word about the healer. Only a meditating or praying person should take part in healing. A healer must have a subtle sensitivity and must realise that all those who come for healing need to be lifted up to God by a process of thought. It would be no good to view the patient, perhaps suffering from many complaints, in a despondent way. There is no condition that comes which cannot be helped, except those of course such as the loss of limbs and deterioration in the brain cells that are past recourse to healing.

So the healer must feel sympathetically for the patient with an optimism that something is going to be achieved. An intimate connection is then built up between the two. The expectant attitude is transmitted to the patient lifting him into the realm of the healer's aura. It enters his heart. In time it becomes a certainty that some amount of good is going to come in and overcome the bad that is there.

The healer should never attempt to heal if he has been greatly upset or has lost his temper with someone, because anything of this nature transfers itself to the patient. He should wait and calm down. It is vital that no negative vibrations should come in.

Now the healer must realise that there are streams of cosmic energy that will flow through his aura to the patient. And he should, for a moment at least, as the healing takes place, be able to register the colours that are needed. Some healers, of course, use coloured lamps, a good thing because they make the patient aware of the colour. And there are also colour charts. Those of artistic persuasion can make their own, so that the patient can see the colour and feel and indeed breathe it in.

If you could see the healer at work from our side you would see the appropriate colour entering in with the breathing of the patient. And you would be conscious of the vital sparking here and there as the hands of the healer come to the part in the physical frame where there is a greater need for the healing power to infiltrate through.

Patients who present themselves for healing should not be encouraged to think of themselves just as physical body. They are body, they are mind, they are spirit - and sometimes there are certain obstacles in the mind. We bring in the heart with the mind here because emotional stress and strain will often retard feeling and the body will always obey what the heart and the mind tell it to do.

The healer should get the patient to treat his body as one with the world of nature. It is the only way to keep it in good repair. All stress and wear comes from fighting the flow of the natural laws. There has to be harmony and balance, so the practitioner of this holistic way should be both priest and doctor, should be able to give good counsel, and should at the same time be able to allow the healing rays to stream through to merge and mingle with the patient's own recuperative powers.

This holistic healing obeys important universal laws and draws on natural processes such as the waves of the sea. They must recede at certain fixed times and they must come in again at certain other times. And the seasons. As the earth turns on its axis, each season must take over in its turn. But every summer is different. There are laws which are fixed and there are laws which allow a vast variety of possibilities to occur, but still within a fixed framework. The alternating night and day. Very fixed laws.

If you enquire within yourselves in a meditative way you will find the rhythmic quality that runs through the seasons entering into you because you live with nature and with its season. You will see how different you are in the spring from the way you are in the summer and autumn and winter. You will begin to realise that, if you are to have the recreative ability to keep your human frame in good formation with your other bodies, you must take advantage of the season you are living in.

The spring is a time of new beginnings, a burgeoning, a blossoming time. Just as in the trees and plant life there is a new sap rising out of the earth, and you find this sap rising in you coming through from the depths of your being. The time for sitting by the fire and for more mental pursuits is departing and there is this feeling of wanting to get out and to clear the body of the toxins that have entered when the blood has been sluggish and everything in the body has toned down to meet the demands of the winter.

As you go forward towards your summer you feel a new sense of being. The sun is challenging you. The sun is bringing new life to you, and you feel yourself going out to greet it. The more regularly you can greet the sun and draw its rays into your being, the more you will build up and store within your body those things you are going to need as you return to the winter. It need not be just the drear cold of the physical experience. You can establish an inner warmth and each night when the retreat comes into sleep, something builds up within you that will bring you into the springtime fully prepared. This is what will happen when you have responded to each season with the whole of your being.

Let us look at the four seasons again in a different aspect. Think of spring as a time for sowing and the preparation of the soul, the young life gradually learning how to grow into a maturity of being. We see him discovering himself to be a person, feeling his feet, seeking out, beginning to understand how he can use his thought processes, bringing in the hands to create and make things, to build with bricks and blocks. The child then uses the heart to feel life quickened with the forming of friendship, through the awareness of the family link, and a feeling for other people existing outside the family boundary. As the spring gradually gives way to summer, the formative processes within the youth have brought the personality into being.

But is not always the case. Within some young people there is a soul conflict, very often brought over from a past incarnation, causing them to miss out on a part of their evolutionary process when it becomes available. This can lead to a lack in the personality that some never transcend. If they were developing harmoniously with the natural life, if they were letting nature really contact them with the creative activity of the godhead realising itself through them, there would be a joy and an optimism established that would overcome all restriction.

So it is with the development of the healing gifts. You are well aware that you are spirit first and foremost, but you need to have a greater consciousness of those many bodies you possess and how they integrate themselves into the fullness of you as a threefold being – and we now speak in terms of the soul, the etheric body and the astral being, which together bring life and motivation to the physical.

We find that the etheric body has powerful links with the cosmos, and also the elemental world with which man has such a strong affinity. But it is most closely linked with the physical body and its consciousness which will, as the cosmos beats down upon it, become more aware of the soul quality that seeks after the three great ideals: beauty, goodness and truth.

It is the etheric body that gives movement and flexibility to the physical frame and to the breathing the full vitality for life. And that brings us to the astral body, the body that shares with the etheric breathing, though it has to breathe in a somewhat different kind of way.

You are conscious sometimes when you draw a very deep breath that somehow you feel more buoyant, more free of the heaviness of the physical body. This is because the astral is fulfilling its function with the etheric. But the astral body is also a body of desire with which you can rove out far from the physical body under special circumstances. The astral body receives from the spiritual impulse, coming through the soul as its intermediary, those desires and thoughts that have a living quality in them.

When they have been brought into being, a man is surrounded by his own creations, his own artistic conceptions. Youth is a great time of seeking after beautiful ideals, with the strong desire there that they shall come into being. But it is important that you continue to dwell on these high ideals throughout your life, bringing to them a greater maturity of purpose. You find that young people often have a very high ideal conception of God and His love. What they do not understand is that love is not an emotion. It goes far beyond emotion. So youth becomes held within the field of emotion, and because the astral or desire body is very sensitive, it is likely to go berserk if the conception of the ideal is not brought into being.

It is here that you get the wrong kind of impulse at work, and instead of the thought forms being those of beauty they become distortions. Whilst they remain, these forms built up have a destructive effect on the life, and there grows within the soul the feeling of cynicism, satire, irony, because the ideals have not worked out as one had beheld them. You see lots of evidence of this in your world, and healers need to understand these things in order to be fully effective.

Now let us introduce another body which not all people need to develop, and that is the psychic body. This body has to learn to grow, to expand, to be as a sheath extending to the senses of the physical frame. It too has close affinities with the astral plane, and the desire body, and is prey to emotionalism. It must therefore be developed with a great deal of care.

Then there is the mental body, a receptacle for the thought-making process and its thought structures. And there is what we call the causal body which runs through that silver cord which links you to the earthly body, the silver cord that is broken only when death comes in.

So you see it is a somewhat complicated piece of machinery that walks about upon the earth. And like any other machinery it needs to be kept in good trim and provided with the right kind of sustenance. That applies to all the bodies, particularly the mental, because as a man thinks today so he becomes tomorrow. And if man is going to stay on the lower instinctual planes of life, satisfying the physical biological needs within him only, he is not going to be able to get into any other body without a desperate struggle to achieve.

You have all seen the low state of the drug addict or the drunkard, which sometimes brings horrific vision to those who succumb. So there is a need to gain mastery over the physical body of earth, the body through which you must manifest, communicate and live the material life.

Now when a breakdown occurs one cannot say that a sudden invasion of the nervous body has come about, because it is no sudden invasion. Things take time to build up and one has to look backwards in order to understand anything. In fact, historically speaking, nothing happens in a moment of time. Even with an accident taking place in the street there were factors at work that led to that accident. So always in every department of life we have to look back and find the cause.

And very often one finds that in seeking the cause one must go back further than the present earth life, probably to a time when, in a previous incarnation, that person inflicted some harm onto somebody else. So this illness has invaded because there is a need to transmute that past condition and change it into power that is good. And healers who are working on a very deep level of spiritual truth will be able to help this process.

Many patients will prove a very severe test for the healer. They are the doubting types. They want to get to grips with life, to feel a meaning or purpose. They are a little above the instinctual levels, just rising up into a desire to cultivate the soul, but they are not strong enough to fully vibrate into this healing ministration.

So what you have got to do is pray for the help to come, and realise that these are the people about whom the Master Jesus said to his disciples, 'Bear ye one another's burdens.' That means you will probably register the pain they are feeling, because you've got to nurse them, you've got to nourish them, and bring them up to a higher state of awareness. And sometimes the healing will be a lengthy process which you must persevere with because they have been sent to you. You are the healer for them. And many times you will perhaps wonder whether you are making much progress with them. You will feel the desperate querying, the doubting coming from them. And there will be a heaviness with you because you are taking it on, you're helping, getting to grips with them on the inner planes.

This inner-plane communication is something which is most important, because until you can meet a person on the inner planes then you won't establish anything vital with him. You can meet in the flesh, you can help him, but this meeting on the inner planes is quite essential. And you will find to your great delight that now and again you can get a person who comes for healing, a true spiritual seeker, an awakening soul, and you know immediately that this one just needs a little spot of help from you and he will be on his way rejoicing.

With some people, healing can have only a very superficial effect - certainly with those who might be seen as the physical clods of earth. You know that you can only heal the physical. You are not going to be able to get into their minds, nor are you going to get to them in a way of spiritual communication. But behind anything that develops in the physical there is always a cause, and you are not going to dismiss that clod of earth, because just coming close to someone where there is dedication and integrity of purpose is going to make a slight indentation into his aura, that in the course of time when he has gone through suffering will become alive within him. But with these people who are so earthy it is hard to achieve much.

Now finally there is magnetic healing. Some people, though not healers in the sense we have been describing, are endowed with a greater life force than others. There is a certain magnetism that is in super-abundance with them. It streams through them, so much so that when they go to visit a sick person in hospital, they just sit on the bed and the patient can feel the waves coming to him, even though he may not be conscious of what is being achieved.

The outpouring of energy that streams towards the earth from the spheres of light is ever seeking to find expression. Its effectiveness depends on many things. It depends on weather patterns, it depends on the aggregate of the emotional phases of the earth plane, and the way the countries are behaving towards each other, and so forth.

Sometimes you find as you go about your tasks on the earth you get weary, you get depleted, you feel that contradictory conditions are being built up within and around you. And we say that the wisest thing to do, particularly if you go to markets, among crowds of people, or to places where there is a lot of noise, when you can get away, perhaps to a garden or natural surroundings, is to visualise the heavenly sun radiating out its warm penetrating rays to you, with the trees and the flowers sending you an energising flow that can heal all the negative vibrations that adversely affect you. And listen to beautiful music, breathe in the rays of peace and contentment, and know yourself within that place of peace as the spiritual being you truly are.

God bless you all.

HEALING: EAST AND WEST

You see around you a world that is not a finished product. It is always in the process of becoming something better. It is true there have been many times throughout history when the world has seemingly crumbled, but always, phoenix-like out of the ashes, there has arisen something that has given elevation to the whole vibration of the earth. And so it is with man himself, always on the way to greater perfection.

And when we come to the vast field of healing, and take a panoramic view of it, we see indeed the great diversity of ways and conditions an individual can find himself within. Some who have sought a spiritual pathway have treated the physical body as if it were of no account. You will have heard of the eastern holy man with his begging bowl sitting by the roadside and holding an arm above his head. He thinks that by so doing he is mortifying the flesh, and through his ascetic longing to walk in the divine way he can bring God alive within himself.

To the westerner this seems a very foolish idea. He looks into the gospels and sees man's body spoken of as a temple of the Lord. He feels that this is an abuse of the physical body, for the arm eventually becomes of no use, and there is the excruciating pain that must be gone through. But the easterner in his make-up is rather different from the man in the west.

We look at the slow, lethargic way in which the eastern world moves. They believe that there is all of eternity to reach perfection. They do not recognise that all have elected to work within a certain plan, and to achieve a certain degree of perfection in this present incarnation, and that by doing so they are serving mankind as a whole.

In the west there is this scurrying about with the anxiety that the whole of the business shall be pushed into the day with hardly a break. It is not generally recognised that quality should be the goal, and that sometimes acceptance of physical and mental inactivity is indeed a positive act.

Here we return to the vital point that the western world would do well to understand, the need to live more in a rhythmic balance of the seasons. The easterner has taken this idea and assimilated it into his being. He is conscious that the soul has its seasons, and he adjusts to each as it comes along. He finds that the clearing, cleansing movements of the spirit do operate, and is thereby led into greater expression of his being. But he accepts that out of his richness, which reaches a zenith according to the needs of his evolutionary process, he must eventually move back into a darkened period once again to gather and prepare for the springtime to come.

In the western world we find man at loggerheads with the seasons as they come about in his soul life. We see certain psychological processes at work within an individual which prevent him from functioning properly. There are perhaps thoughts rising up too dominantly, so that when he should be experiencing the spring he has slipped back into the darkness of winter. And so, more and more, the westerner is looking towards the east to find a way that can lead into a harmony and balance, and a way of looking at life that is more in tune with the world of nature.

A healer at the time of Jesus always took the soul rhythms into account. The Master himself was able to look within the soul of man and see the movements that were taking place. He could see how it was becoming important that this soul should receive an outpouring of power that would help remove an obstruction that had been there for perhaps many years. And he looked for a certain content within the mind of the patient that would tell him whether that one would be able to give up some form of living that had led him into that illness, or whether he would be unable to stand the new light that the Master could shed on the pathway for him.

Throughout the gospels you get this foreknowledge

that resided within the being of the Master. This is what healers should seek to have - a real feeling for the soul progress of the patient, a real willingness to enter into and identify with him, for a short space of time, in order to understand what is already beginning to rise up within that one, but which without the healer's help could not easily be dealt with.

Man is a complex being. Sometimes things within his astral self try to get through and invade the etheric, and when this happens it is very difficult to seperate. Very often in the outworking of an invasion there come periods of great passivity within the patient. He cannot seem to get to grips with life. In fact, there seems to be no desire for life at all. And sometimes we see there is an unholy war taking place between mind and etheric and astral, and the disturbance may be producing some obstruction, such as cancer, within the physical body, which will have to be removed.

Now when this occurs there is a falling apart of the life forces within the personality, and it is at this point that eastern and western methods meet - because if the patient is going to come out of this condition then the seat of desire within the astral body (which is more closely linked with the soul than the other bodies) must first receive a stimulation.

When your eastern healer gets to work he concentrates very vitally on the restoration of the astral/soul balance, so that the soul can receive from the spirit, restoring a wholeness to all the bodies. He knows that as the physical gradually becomes recharged with power, so the etheric will begin to resume a normal function. He knows too, because of his occupation with the seasons, that one cannot go faster than one is able. There has got to be the sowing of new seeds of hope within the patient before the fruits can begin to be seen. And once he has got a balance there, then he must reach the mind of the patient, which needs to find its clear linking through with the astral and soul bodies. He will enter into the lengthy process of striving to communicate on the inner levels with the patient.

When you look at the healer in the western world you find that he is very anxious that the streams of energy shall just rush through him and into the patient, to disperse at once that which has taken such a long time to come about. He will probably have to work hard to instill confidence in the mind of the patient for this cannot be maintained easily through any lengthy process. There will be the doubt in the mind of the healer, as well as the patient. We often see, even with healers who have gone through a full period of training and who are, as they should be, aspirants on the spiritual path, an inability to look back into the past to see what brought this into the physical frame. No illness starts today and is here tomorrow.

In the east, man is more deeply rooted in the past. He has not shaken the dust from the soles of his feet, as it were, and cannot relate what is happening to the present time. He has the ability to look straight through into the future, ignoring the present, and although this is a mistaken process, yet there is light that streams from the past which can help the easterner build up for the future, in spite of his inability to deal with the present.

The western temperament often wants to push the past away as though it were something that had not happened. He is able to live in the present and work for the future, but that future is not so delineated, because he is not willing to let the past be present with him. So when you come to the process of healing, the easterner, through being so entrenched in the past, is able to have a quickened understanding and bring his mind into focus through his imagination to feel after the future. He can see the patient as responding and more alive. The western healer concentrates on the blackness of the present health condition. He cannot see the full process of health succumbing to illness then moving back into health.

The ideal should be a willingness to face the past, all the unpleasantness, that allows the healer to get to grips with the cause of the illness so that he can then gently lead the patient along to the point where the patient sees where his fault lies and how it came about. This is sometimes a long, painful process, because most people tend to run away from anything unpleasant.

The healing should be augmented by prayers offered, and the smallest light that is shed on the future must be reported to the patient, always with sensible optimism. We often watch the interaction of patient and healer, but we do not so often see this ready entering into soul communication that is needful, which brings words to the patient, words to the healer, so that they can work together, so that the patient can get the glimpse of a future state of wholeness for himself, so that he will enquire: "What am I to do with my life?"

We all too often find that after the obstruction is removed the patient slips back into an old way of life and thought. The hates, greeds, sensualities are carried forward into the future, and this is a breeding ground for more disease to come. But increasingly society is recognising that healing can provide hope where previously there was none. This will open the way whereby those with psychic vision fully awake will be able to look into the past, the present and the future of the patient. And the next 50 years will see the full acceptance of such people by the orthodox scientific and medical fraternities.

But first the fear must be eliminated which clouds man's ability to see his true co-operative nature. He must come into a much more alive understanding of the world in which he lives, and enter into a wholeness of being within himself that can safeguard and protect. We have known of people who have plunged into icy seas and have been able to withstand the immense cold. These things can happen to anyone walking in the pathway. You will find that as the need of the moment is, so the power will come to you, and the fears and anxieties will not hold you in their thrall.

Insecurity is a world-wide thing, fed by the banks of negativity that exist because man has ensouled unloving thought forms. Think of all the wrong states that have been within the world, the wars, the hideous crimes. These give rise to monster-like shapes which haunt the earth. So we see that the antidote to fear is faith.

You must learn to appreciate this beautiful world, one

19

that is in the process of becoming it is true, but a world which you can still register within your being, each one, a world with which your soul can identify. It takes work, much endeavour, a willingness to look at yourself completely. Not a mad rush and a scramble - nor the too slow gazing at the sunset of the easterner. There is a need that east and west shall meet, and in that meeting the best that is in both shall come through and give ample aid to each other.

God bless you all.

THE PRIMARY RAYS

So many people are thinking along the lines of colour healing today. You have got away from the drab colours of the past. There is a great choice, and many new colours will come as the New Age progresses that are closer to the colours upon the spiritual plane. It is needful for the purification of the earth to take place on much higher levels than hitherto, and not only are these new colours required, but also a higher awareness on the part of the healers in order that they will be used in the right way. You would not put yourself in the hands of an untrained surgeon, now would you?

Many who are becoming more aware of a feeling for the New Age, the pioneers, know that they can join in the dance of the cosmic radiations. When we look at these cosmic energies we see that they are in a constant state of movement, a swirling. They are performing a dance, like the fireworks that give off the sparks, the beautiful colours going off in all directions, radiating down towards the earth.

At present only the developed clairvoyant can see this, but by using your imagination you can certainly open yourself up to the influence of these radiations in a more realistic way. Begin with an exercise that opens you out to the sun, using your mind to envisage the sun that gives life to the earth. But keep at the back of your mind the spiritual sun, without which the sun of earth could have no life at all. As you open your being to the sun, draw down the rays, see them penetrating your heart, and then you will feel the loosening of the heavy doors that seem to be between you and your inner self. Through the whole of your being you are being raised.

Now, what about the meaning of the colours? If you investigate widely, you will no doubt discover a bewildering variety of different theories and systems for the colour healing. There is no right way. You are all unique people. You only have to look at the human face to know that. And so it is with groups of people. Each will receive according to the ray that is being transmitted from the Hierarchal Lord who is in charge of it on the inner planes. Not all teachers agree therefore and so you get this cult and that cult, forcefully presented sometimes where there is not the recognition of the necessity of this difference and the necessity that all systems should co-exist harmoniously. Seek and find the group and the way that is for you.

We shall now give some thoughts on colour which might stimulate you along new avenues of exploration. You find that in the world of nature green is a predominant colour. Man has made this the colour for safety. It is the colour for balance, midway between the earth and the spheres. It has its own particular musical intonation, as indeed has every colour, and when you feel out of gear with yourself, moody and restless, then you should strive to cloak yourself with green. We refer particularly to the beautiful, fresh grass green, the green of the new young leaves as they come into being. Try to absorb that colour, and it is a good idea to breathe it in through your nostrils, a long deep breath. See it going to your solar plexus and you will rapidly get more into stride with yourself.

Another colour that is particularly good for the nervous system is the violet - the beautiful shade that comes with what you call the African violet. When you feel nerve tension building up within you, what you could do is to lie flat on your back and see the violet hovering above you. Breathe it in. Feel it entering in at the nerve junctures where one nerve system joins up with another, first the crown of the head, then the throat, the nape of the neck, the solar plexus and the base of the spine. See it passing through the whole of your body. If you do this properly, you should feel a wondrous warmth and a tingling that extends right into your hands and right down to your feet.

Use the wonderful gift that God has given of being able to visualise; and remember that you can only learn to see clearly through training the mind. This is essential. You get hundreds of opportunities in your daily lives to do this. Your lot is thrown perhaps in a business field, working alongside people who rub you up the wrong way. You have to strive to be placid, to pull yourself up when your thoughts stray into negative patterns. You must create an inner world of positive thought. You must be master and mistress in the household of your mind.

Daily you have access to the divine Eg(g)o within you – quite apart from that silly ego of the earth. We purposely call it a divine Eg(g)o, because that is soft. It speaks of the power of spirit. And daily you are building into this Eg(g)o the sort of person you are, because that is what you are going to take back to the world of spirit when the physical body has at last to go back to the earth.

To return to our colours. We want to speak next of orange. You all know the value of oranges in the system, and indeed if you catch a cold or chill and you take the orange juice, not eating for twenty-four hours, then you find that the cold does not attack you quite so much. Orange, indeed, is the colour of vitality and of strength. You need this colour when you are going through a period of weakness, whether in the form of an inability to concentrate, or through a weakness in the physical body.

If it is the former, then visualise orange in front of you and place a band of it completely around the head. Do this pouring your thought into it – and mind you, these exercises are not easy. You have got to live into them, get a grip on them. Spirit living is the most arduous kind of living that you can envisage. See the band of orange gradually becoming expanded, completely covering the head. There will be a certain kind of feeling associated with this that you will recognise.

If it is a weakness in the physical body, then a right way to get your orange is to see it coming in as rays that penetrate through the earth, that come through the feet right up to the solar plexus. And for this it is once again

23

best done flat on the back. Ten minutes should be ample, though with practice this can be reduced to five. But you must do it intensely. You cannot just weakly think of it and let other thoughts come in. You have got to hang on to the thought. You have got to build the image properly – and you will find you will get back a renewal of energy.

The next colour we want to talk about is yellow, a colour of the intellect, an inspirational, intuitional colour also, a very good colour to dwell upon at the beginning of a meditation exercise. Feel this field of yellow above you and try to elevate yourself into it. When you are meditating properly, that is what happens. You don't feel it happening in your physical body so much, but in the soul body. This soul body is being raised up, and you may sometimes feel this, particularly when sitting in group meditation. This is nothing to get alarmed about. It is simply that your psychic self has expanded and is making you feel this elevation of the astral and soul body.

Particularly with those of you who are creative artists in some way, when you feel that your muse has deserted you and you are somewhat barren of inspiration, use the yellow. Do a meditation on it. You will be surprised what it can do for you. But again, you've got to really do it with a will.

Now we come to blue. Oh, how many shades of blue there are. There is the beautiful sparkling blue, the sapphire. This colour soothes pain. If you have a pain somewhere in your body, first tell yourself that you can overcome this pain. Visualise this beautiful translucent blue, drawing it to you at the spot where the pain is. And that goes for mental anguish as well as physical pain – that which comes into the mind when one has to face up to some difficult, desperate situation.

Next we come to red. Red – Mars – fighting – wars. But you couldn't do without red, the colour of the blood. We can also think of fire as warm, revivifying, and as something that burns, too. Sometimes in an illness there should be a burning out, and for this red is useful. You all know those awful diseases such as cancer growths within the human body. In this new age that is coming the red, the beautiful colour of blood, will be used to burn them out. And when you've burnt something out, you need a soothing colour to follow. You just can't allow the red ray to penetrate through the body without bringing in the glowing pink afterwards.

The red should be envisaged as coming through the crown of your head and out through your fingertips to the seat of the illness. Or it can be seen as being drawn by you down from above the patient, actually taking it with your fingers. It is good to enact these things. You have to make them a reality. This also applies when you treat yourself.

When you are out in the spirit planes on your nightly journeys you are being shown many things, because in the present time you are being trained to be the healers of the future. We see so many healers on the earth disregarding the necessity for a better understanding of healing, caught up in their own egos, rushing out to do it all unprepared. It is very foolish. One needs to know a little bit about the human body, and the human emotions. One needs to know how to protect oneself. This is learnt in the sleep state mainly. And of course you are being taught to heal yourselves because your power as a healer is only present to the extent that you can love yourself as a divine instrument of God's love. You cannot do for others what you cannot do for yourself.

We are sure some of you have come back and in the morning remembered having seen lovely colours, remembered having been with people, some of whom you have been helping while out of the body. (This memory can be cultivated if you wish.) The more you are outwardly occupied, active, striving to accomplish and bringing relief to the earth and its peoples, so more you will find it is a necessity to keep your contact with the spirit worlds through meditation and in circles of development.

There is one shade of blue you call indigo. That is very good for the ears. Some people suffer from head noises which could be a catarrhal inflammation of the eardrums, or those buzzings and noises experienced by older people when going towards deafness. Concentrate upon the indigo ray, see it entering the ear. Bring it down with your hands if you feel you can get it through better that way, and see it going right through the ear to work deeply into the condition. You will find this very helpful.

And what about black? Some say you should never use this colour in healing. It is associated with depression, with black magic and with death. There is a time, however, when it can be used. On the large scale, after a war, the black is very necessary to help clear away the destruction before the light can beam forth again. Black absorbs light and focuses it, more inwardly, at a seat of great need. But when mixed with other colours, perhaps in conjunction with a brown, you get the dirty colours found in wartime, fields of energy building up so often on a dirty, darkish red, that awful red we spoke of, which brings in the fighting principle, but the wrong kind of fight.

Beyond the dark, though, there is always the light of the spiritual sun available to you, which can only be obstructed by clouds of your own making.

God bless you all.

THE SPECIALIST COLOURS

Many systems of colour healing give very fixed meanings to each ray. This restricts their use, and healers who expect to see a particular range of colours in the aura will see nothing but those colours. They will develop a kind of psychic colour-blindness. It is a good idea to read the various books on the subject, but not good to allow them to override one's own sensitivity to shade and meaning.

There are certain illnesses that respond more favourably to some colours, it is true, but it does depend on the individual and the particular stage of development of the illness. There are complex gradations of colour, each having its own particular note, much the same way as the homoeopathic remedies come in different subtle strengths.

A person who is seriously ill with cancer may need the fiery orange so that the growth can be burnt out of his body, while a person with that disease still in its infancy may require the beautiful pain-killing sapphire blue. What a healer must do is to keep expectations right out of conscious interference, holding the mind in readiness to receive intuitively the colour appropriate for this stage of the condition presenting itself.

Because the souls coming forward now have bodies with that little bit more of the etherial quality the healing process is constantly being refined. Healers are needed who can relate to the subtleties that are there, who are much more sensitive to these higher notes and hues, and who can help release karmic conditions now causing physical disturbance, which the healer of yesterday would have been unable to reach.

People are becoming more colour-conscious, in their clothing, wearing one colour today and a different one tomorrow as the need changes, and in their homes. This is helping the healers. Men not so long ago wore mainly grey and brown suits. Grey is a very neutral colour and some shades one should not use at all, but the very light grey is good when the individual is going through something he cannot get to grips with in his life, the understanding is not there, grey can help. Place a robe of the colour around and feel the stimulation that will lead to a sense of peace.

And brown. Again this is a colour that is not usually very helpful. You go into a brown study, or get browned off. But there is a good kind of brown, the light tan shade that you find when the leaves turn. This corresponds to a quietude, a confidence. It is not a colour that can lift you soaring to the heavens, but it is a colour of contentment, one that helps you to place your feet firmly on the ground. And there is that lovely clay colour that comes with the darker soil. It too belongs specifically with the earth, and if sometimes you feel yourself getting carried away, and you need to ground yourself more, this is a very good colour to use. See it coming into the solar plexus and down. It is not a colour that goes up.

The drab uniform of the past has moved into the blue-jean uniform of the present young. If only they knew, particularly the belligerent rebels, what lies behind this unlovely dress. It is the sackcloth and ashes, the need for retribution speaking through them. The blue, of course, comes from Egypt, and harks back to the misuse of power that stems from those far-off times. There is not the full vibrant colour, but the deliberate fading, the shabby condition.

Does this not speak of the need to bring in something of lost purity? Most of you have brought back the corruption from one of the phases of Egyptian folly, and you must work with it until it has been eased from your personal and group soul. But there is a growing feeling for change now, a wish to return to the quality of the proper blue, to the dignity, the devotion, and the right following in the occult pathway, with the vision alive and alight.

The Egyptian blue is used, as it is so often in healing, in helping to clear the physical effects of this karma.

There is more feeling now for the Chinese blue, which belongs almost completely to healing in its widest sense, for the soothing of distressed states, and for the gathering of the inharmonious strains in man's being, in nature and in music, blending these into a greater harmony. And the cobalt blue, raying out from that high spiritual centre, the Amazon Basin, to soothe the troubled minds of men.

Very many of the healing colours are linked to natural forms, not just pink, but coral pink, or rose pink. Each has its own particular quality of association. The beautiful rose pink, so important to the Rosicrucians, is perhaps the most spiritual colour affinity known to man.

Since the dawn of man the precious stones and gems with their affinities to the rhythms of the planetary zodiac and the seasons have been known to have healing and occult properties. There is the amethyst ray, blending with the heart, particularly the glorious rose amethyst, which is a prayer for the wounded spirit, a colour for compassion.

It is necessary to meditate long in order to gain a full understanding of how colour links up with nature and to earn the right to combine and use some of these more refined colours on those souls who have in some way strayed from the path, and who need the specialist's skill.

There is the pearl ray of rejuvenation, the ray that breaks up the rigidities in man that would result in a gradual breakdown in the proper functioning, where the muscles lose elasticity, the metabolism becomes sluggish, and the body begins to look older than its years. But consider how much more effective this colour can be when used in conjunction with the pink.

Then we have the silvery ray which really only works in support of other colours. There is the silvery blue, the silvery grey, the silvery pearl, the silvery amethyst. It is a colour that can be very effective when dealing with the split personality - not the psychiatric version, but where an unwanted element from a past life has invaded the personality and caused it to be other than what it should be. Here the silvery mauve can be introduced. See it entering in where the pineal gland is, and working its way through the body, then this unwanted intrusion can be driven back out of influence.

Mauve is the colour of aspiration. You all have had occasions when thoughts just do not come, when words make little sense, or when you have sat down to pray and the heart seems dead, and you need to lift yourself out of this for the clarity and feeling to come. Mauve is a good prayer colour. Visualise it coming through the crown of the head and down to the heart. And when you establish contact for absent healing, it can be good to first place the patient in the mauve light seeing him bright and smiling and rising above his condition.

Now the silver is also used in conjunction with the Chinese blue around the solar plexus, particularly where there has been some psychic disturbance. If you have to go into harsh surroundings you can protect yourself by seeing this beautiful Chinese blue coming and spinning a web right over the solar plexus. If you have to confront someone and hostility is there, see the blue with the silver darts blending in. Silver is also useful for the polarisation of the various bodies.

And what about gold, that high spiritual colour, yet linked to a metal that men fight over. Gold oversees the stability of the world's economies, and will be even more influential in this regard in years to come. Precious it is, and yet abused. It is a colour that should be used with care when called down from the spiritual heights. There is a price to pay for its misuse.

Gold is a symbol of high endeavour. It is selfless service, where one gives and counts not the cost, fights and heeds not the wounds. Joan of Arc links most closely with this ray. It is a martyr's colour really. And in lesser ways, when you've got to put aside concerns of self and carry a weaker brother or sister, the gold of selfless service would come in there. When used in healing it can be linked to the sun, the source of all life, and be used to bring in the Christ power of transcendence.

Then there is the copper ray, so useful in arthritic conditions, and a new ray that will have great significance in the New Age as healers learn how to work with it, the steel. When you think of what goes into the making of steel you will begin to appreciate its special qualities as a ray of great penetration and refinement. It is linked to a rod of power stretching down from the higher planes, and while the pearl ray is more linked to the gradual dispersal of conditions, the steel ray will enter in and burn out. It will in time replace the surgeon's knife.

The pearl ray modifies gradually. It is a quiet, manoeuvring influence that gradually brings things together, things that have been severed or broken, nerves that have become frayed. But sometimes more drastic measures are needed and the steel ray is brought in. This can bring about conditions for a time in the person which seem far worse than before. This is why it should only be used by healers of great sensitivity and experience. But after the patient has patiently gone through the application of the steel, the pearl ray will take over and bring in the harmonious quality to work on what has been aroused into activity by the steel. The two are complimentary. And afterwards, the pink ray is often sent in to harmonise and subdue.

Those who administer the steel ray can also direct it into the atmospheric pollution that is blocking the way for many of the other rays to effectively get through to the earth. Because steel is modified by man, the elementals enter into the picture. They are always around in any healing situation, but particularly when these special rays are being used. The pearl ray is associated with the airy elementals and the steel with the elementals of the earth.

But what of the future? We have said that a more subtle appreciation of colour is now needed, and healers can become sensitive to the supportive colours that work in between the main colours of the spectrum. Some have been mentioned. The rose pink comes before the red, and the cobalt blue between the red and the orange, with magenta coming between the orange and the yellow.

The function of these colours is to bring in a greater amplifying power for the cosmos. They are the scavengers, taking away that which is dust-laden, and keeping it out of the field of the rainbow colours. They have their own potency when used in healing, too, but they are not required so frequently, most often to subdue the more strident effects of the main colours.

As the pace of the planet quickens, new colours will come in on the healing and cleansing wavelengths. There is an eighth colour of the rainbow gradually appearing. It has always been there, but only now are people becoming aware of it. It is more the puce, a sort of red going into mauve. The electrical charges increasing in the atmosphere have brought it forward into prominence. It is, of course, linked to the eighth level of evolution, that of service at its highest, personal sacrifice, a quality so necessary at this time for the upliftment of the planet. The ninth colour will begin to make its presence felt some time next century, linked to the final stage of purification that advanced mankind will have to undergo in order to transcend the need to incarnate.

The psychically aware will have advance sight of the colours of the spheres beyond, that are more beautiful than any available to the earth senses, as they begin to flow into the earth. As precise colour becomes more needed in healing and the arts, group healing and group creativity will become more established. Every healer must come into a deeper understanding of colour, through meditation and visualisation. Think upon each hue. Allow it to reveal its secrets to you. Allow colour to work through you in every area of your life, and you will truly be able to heal and soothe this troubled earth.

God bless you all.

THE WAY OF ATTUNEMENT

It is with a very real endeavour to place ourselves at the service of you earth children that we come back to your world, benighted as it is, in order that you might have the experience of an attunement with us.

First we would like to mention the great noise. You are conscious of a great deal of noise that is unnecessary, your speeding two-wheeled vehicles that give off at times a most ferocious sound and the noise of machinery, particularly your drills used in road construction. You have many noises that echo around you because of man's distress with himself, the noise of arguments and the grumbling expressions of discontent. All these things bring stress and strain into your physical body. Yet we do agree that some of the noise is a necessary evil.

How is man to cope in such a noisy world reflecting, as it so often does, the noise within his own soul? It is in the battle-ground of the soul that discordance first arises and unless man can bring a panacea into this discordance he will not live comfortably in his bodies.

When a battle is in progress between the noise that man is making within himself and that atmosphere of peace and harmony striving to come in, there will be a period of time when man's bodies seem out of gear - and if man is going to accomplish the alignment of his bodies then he needs to draw into himself a rhythmic process.

Now you know the nerves of the physical body are very delicate things, easily upset. But you see some people as having nerves of steel. Perhaps you envy them. How is it that they have this calm composure? But sometimes this is with a person who does not recognise any spirituality in his being. Many martial figures have created chaos under the banner of peace and many religious leaders have been hypnotised by power while professing their allegiance to

God. How could those of the Spanish Inquisition do what they did unless they had these nerves of steel?

So we see that the powers of opposition, which are working hard in every department of life, must enter even into the field of the arts, including the music. For it is upon the waves of hard, harsh, difficult vibrations that these souls who persevere in the way of discordance, with their nerves of steel, are able to exercise the things that bring so much grief and pain and suffering to the children of earth.

Then there are those intrepid souls who, though they would confess to feeling very nervous within themselves, do not fail at the crucial moment. They go forward to save a life, should a life be in danger. They grapple with conditions wherein a crisis state reigns. They stand up to those who seek to bring in the discordance. They are able to do this because of the harmony within their own soul life.

Any troubled state upon your earth is a condition that needs healing. When war breaks out it is a rising up of so many past conditions, wherein there is music that is unholy, that have now come to a crescendo, and this music has got to be changed by those who are willing to come in and divest it of its power to disrupt. And so the peace bringers, the heavenly chorus of the invisible spheres, are forever discharging into the atmosphere of earth the harmonies that man can receive and use if he is willing.

Sometimes when trouble is at work you find people will group themselves together. They are aware of the disharmony entering in and taking charge of so many souls upon your earth, souls who are not aware of being hypnotized by these discordant echoes, and they wish to help them.

When a group comes together for peace and healing, they may decide to help give expression to what they are trying to achieve by having their own particular piece of music. We might call it their signature tune. And they will very often open and close their meetings with this tune. This is very good, for we who strive to bring order into chaos are able to endow their song with rhythms of our own, and bring in, too, the appropriate colours for these rhythms. This will help bring accord to their efforts.

There is a great need for times of group attunement. In your centres, your churches, people coming together and entering into a soul relationship one with the other, they become conscious sometimes of feeling themselves to be larger than they know, not in any way feeling bumptious or proud about it, but having the realisation that something vital has entered into their midst and is beginning to have a soul life of its own. And this does happen. It is happening here tonight. There is always an oversoul established when people gather together regularly for service, and that oversoul has its own particular keynote.

There are always a number of spirit entities from the spheres linked to that oversoul who will be a big source of support, with their inspiration and strength coming through to the group. Now you know that very often people come together with the very best of intentions, and there is great harmony and peace between them when the work is started, but soon there come the disagreements, because perhaps one wants to be, as you say, top dog. Another will say, 'Oh no, I don't think we should do that, we should do this,' and all sorts of disharmonies enter in. Now what should one do?

Many people feel if they have a discord, 'Oh well, we'll disband.' But that is very foolish behaviour. There is a way that all the stresses and strains between people can be ironed out, by attunement. But the leader of the group must take on the responsibility to achieve it.

It is necessary for the leader to sit alone or with a favoured companion and once they have got within that inner citadel they should visualise each member of that group as coming into a room with them. They must mentally speak to each one of the responsibility that he bears as a member of the group, must arouse within him a desire to fit into a co-operative effort and that if his particular pet thing is not being done immediately, well a little later on perhaps it can come into being. But he must be willing that somebody else's pet idea shall be worked upon.

And by this linking up through pure imagination, working on thought levels, each member will begin to feel he must settle more completely within the group, that he really is an active and valued participant.

Sometimes a person coming into a group is made to feel a sleeping partner, as it were, is hardly acknowledged. Perhaps the leader has thought, 'Ah we have a dullard here, we won't pay much attention to this one.' Now this is not good. The dullard has been attracted to the group because of some need, because something within him has got to be aroused, so that he feels he has a definite place - and some little responsibility should be put upon his shoulders by the leader of the group.

You see, one needs to understand, to have a sort of psychological know-how of how to build up successfully these relationships that go so sadly astray. We have often known one who has come as a dullard into a group being so roused that some gift that has lain dormant has suddenly begun to blossom. It is karma working itself out, because groups do not come together willy nilly on the earth. There is a law of attraction in operation drawing this one to this group and that one to that group, because in the far past the members have been together and there have been many things that they have failed to achieve. And now perhaps three, four hundred years later here is another opportunity for them to work together and overcome. And what do such groups achieve?

They establish a link with the Solomon's Temple of Wisdom that is on the borders between the astral plane and the earth. For each group has its own particular place, its own particular name, it's own particular colour, and these become manifest. And the earth plane itself becomes a little more purified, a little more cleansed of the stains, of the guilt of past ages, because groups are being formed here and there that are responding with a sincerity of purpose. Even the little home circles meeting, three or four people perhaps, these are all paving the way whereby the illumined ones can come in and purify the whole vibration of the earth. And a time of attunement is required each and every time they meet.

It would be good if you could find the keynote of your group, but you first have to find the rhythm and the note within yourselves. There are many ways of doing this - but we will give a simple way because it will be better understood.

You can think of your feet as being Doh, and you may think of your lower leg above the ankles as being Re and your knees as Mi. Your thighs are Fah, your solar plexus is Soh, your heart is La, your throat is Ti and the crown of your head is Doh. We want you to experience something quite important as you do it.

Breathe in and sing the Doh - and as you sing it let your mind send it to the feet, where it should vibrate and bring in a feeling of buoyancy. Hold onto it until it feels complete. And so on through the scale to the top of your head. Your own keynote is the one which resonates most strongly.

When you get tired of dealing with these discordant notes, the sounds that would cause you to fret or make you disorganised within yourself, do this exercise and you will begin to breathe in that rhythmic process that can help your bodies come into alignment.

And we would especially give this to people who have to live with noise, people who have the beat of the popular music around them during their working life and those who must be near these atrocious drill machines. If you can encourage them to do this exercise after they have left their job, then you will be doing them a great service.

Man can be a conqueror in any field he chooses. But you get sometimes those souls who feel that there is no music in them. They have not the musical ear, they say. And when they start to sing, they find that instead of uttering the sweet harmonies they are off key. Why is this? How has someone no ear for music when he is a rhythmic being? It is not as it should be. This person must find his keynote, where it resides, and really try to get the rhythmic process properly to work within him.

Now we would like to mention the planets. As you may realise each planet has a particular keynote (with its subdivisions) and these keynotes are in colour applicable to the planet. Everybody is born under a certain birth sign and planet, and at times when the powers of opposition are very strong around you, to be able to have music with the particular colour and keynote of your birth sign is most helpful. There are always powers of opposition that would seek to get in and disrupt and keep you from walking in the spiritual path. The music is bringing you back to realising your unity with the music of the universe that echoes from the cosmos.

The earth is a great entity. You would not say that you live on an earth that is perfect, unblemished. You pollute the air, you pollute the earth and the earth has a karma to work out and you are linked with that karma. So by realising you are part of the great musical dance of the cosmos you can help the earth, help it to prepare for the time when the desert is going to blossom as the rose - and the lion will lie down with the lamb.

Your earth was brought into being by a sound, a note of creation, as indeed you were. So we see how important the true sound within man is. And now we want to deal with something that is often very much misunderstood, the sound of silence. Silence is golden, you say, and so it is. Silence brings that particular colour into being.

When man is deep in meditation, he is hearing his soul. He is bringing in a balance between the spirit being that he is, and his soul. And this sound within the silence is the keynote of the creative world that brought him into being. It will echo within his soul as he enters into that more transcendental meditation, helping him to find the God within himself and to enter with his own note into the sound of creation.

God bless you all.

SOUND AND MUSIC

When you think of spirit you cannot think of form, but you can think of light. And as you let your mind dwell on the light, form seems to come about within it, form that pulsates with power and energy. Now what causes this pulsation? It is many of the sounds which emanate from the spheres. Some of those higher in the scale of musical vibrations bring a scintillation into that body of light which will lead to an upliftment being felt throughout the whole being in any person who is aware and striving to cultivate the spiritual part of himself.

You have heard mention of the music of the spheres, and each of the spheres has its own intonation according to that which it is working upon at any given time. When we speak of healing with musical vibrations, we also include the world of nature where we have to deal with and understand the many undesirable elements that invade the natural world, which seek to impinge and bother the body of man, the notes that bring in the discordant, strident, harsh echoes.

Music must be harmonious and this music that emanates from the spheres as it comes down through the various planes is added to by the workers on these planes who strive to clear unwelcome conditions within the atmosphere of the earth.

In the music of the spheres, in the cosmic radiations, there are of course these melodies that emerge, nature's own music. And man's whole body is a vibrational scale. Various parts of the body correspond to various chords. Musicians in a future time will be very happy to come and play the required note so that it can go through the healer to the patient. And we will use the human voice, which can bring release especially when people come together to sing.

Choirs will be sent into hospitals and mental hospitals to harmonise all the discordant notes caused by the depressions and the fears of the coming surgery. And sometimes the choirs from the invisible spheres do visit your hospitals, striving to bring in the harmony, so that souls can come into a real preparation. All the various organs that have come for treatment need a different sound. And every condition can be aided by attunement to a choir, a singing team, which has come in, lifting the vibrations of the patient so that he can feel and benefit from the harmonic influence present within all healing.

Some people, particularly those who are psychically aware, certainly do hear the music of the spheres, responding in a clairaudient way, but others need to get into a meditative state that reaches up to the higher planes. With the usual kind of meditation you do not rise very far in the scale of gradations from the earth towards the spirit realms. But there is a plane that we would call the Hierarchal plane from which the teachings and all the inventions and the creative genius flow through to the earth plane. So when you think about the music of the spheres, and you carry the thought in your heart that you would like to hear this music, you can certainly make the conditions conducive to it. You say: 'Now perhaps tonight when my body is quiet and I am about to slip into sleep, God willing I might be open to it.' Never assert your own will. Always it must be handed over to the spiritual Will, and if you do it patiently, persistently, we are quite sure you can open yourself up to this divine music of the spheres.

The earth itself can be very sick. The earth can be a breeding ground for hostilities, all kinds of wrong things proceeded with, and we are dependent upon the children of earth who are willing to co-operate so that those of us in the realm of spirit who are the clearers of the atmosphere can work effectively around the earth's aura to prevent disasters coming into being.

When a disaster occurs on the earth it is because the harmonious element is missing. Discordant, chaotic echoes have entered and have, for a time, over-ruled the harmonious, soothing waves that could come in and bring peace, and the power that peace endows the atmosphere with.

When you walk into a place where people are grouped together and they are striving to work for a good cause, you are conscious of this element of uplift. You can feel it rippling around you. You feel it is good for you to be there taking in the atmosphere. This is because, in the unconscious depths of yourself, you are registering the musical note from the sphere where these people are working together in sympathy and in harmony. But there are those occasions when you go into a group of people and you do not feel that. There are jagged conditions. What should you do there?

You should at once vibrate to the harmony within, that peaceful element that can emanate from you. You think of some particular musical instrument that you like and a piece of music for that instrument and allow that music to be drawn in through the solar plexus. Use the imaginative equipment with which you are certainly endowed. Get the tune going in your mind, and then feel it going to your solar plexus and from there right out into the atmosphere, striving to overcome this discord.

You are entering into an age when imagination is going to be a very strong influence. It always has been but men have not been aware of it. Music must have a form when you think of the notes. But music comes in beautiful swirling forms of light, in circles, in loops, and it irradiates the whole atmosphere. It is like a fountain of sound cascading over people. In times to come you will be sent into many places in order to quell rebellions as a channel bringing in the soothing, harmonising vibrations of spirit to overcome the harsh, discordant echoes.

And you can imagine how as you become more able to to meditate in colour you will go into these places using this technique and you will feel the softening effect, because when one brings in the harmony of the spheres people who are at loggerheads feel the hypnotic spell.

With so much hostility and dissension in the world around you at this present time, is it any wonder that you are experiencing so much difficulty in your personal

41

lives? This is very good soul training for you, however, to have to grapple with conditions and vibrations where sometimes your back is up against the wall, because it brings out from the unconscious depths a stability, an understanding, a resourcefulness you did not know you possessed.

Now let us look at some specific cases where music can heal. First the nerve problems. Sometimes the music is around the patient in a very direct sense. And sometimes it is there, but only coming through the spirit operators who are around. And as the music operates, it brings its own colour with it. When we are working with a depressed patient overwhelmed with fears and anxieties we bring in a mixing of the green and the violet shades which results in a more purple element influencing the condition. Here we always enter into the solar plexus, and very often the healer can get the correct colour in his mind and so assist in the process. He will see this rising up to occupy the brain centre, and the mind of the patient, thereby bringing to him a feeling of release.

Of course we do not say that all can be accomplished in a moment of time, but the more you succeed in understanding how music and colour play their part in healing, the more it will endow you with greater insight.

Many healers know that something is definitely happening when they lay the hands on, that some discharge of power is taking place, but they are content to leave it at that. The healer who understands, and who is in tune with the healers from the spirit world, will respond more precisely to the musical vibration that is being set up. He will hear this is his mind, and he will know where to apply it and for how long, because sometimes one must hold onto a note until it has accomplished a dispersal.

You must be alive, very positive in your mind when healing. We deplore it when we see just the putting on of the hands, with the thoughts of the healer many miles away. The thoughts should be with the patient. It is good to have some light banter, but the mind must be there, so that there is the stronger identification of healer and patient.

Sometimes the nervous element brings in what you call insomnia. Many people find that at night they are awake and thinking of all the things they haven't done, or the old worries of the past. Again there is a simple process we recommend which works in a rhythmic way and comes in with the breath.

Take a few deep breaths and then think of music you are very fond of, something with words and music. 'The Lord is my shepherd' is very good for people of a religious disposition. Or a lullaby. No-one is too old for these. With awareness, you breathe the music deeply into yourself. On each breath the music will further relax you as the spirit becomes more co-operative and the deep-seated tensions gradually depart. It may not work straight away, particularly if you've had a difficult day, but it helps you overcome this intrusive thinking about things that causes tension and restlessness, and in time it will have a salutary effect. The colours to be used are the violet for the nerves and indigo to bring relaxation into the organs.

Also with tension headaches, or with mental fatigue, the creative endeavour overdone, a soothing lullaby can work wonders. 'Sweet and Low' is good, or something similar, and as you hear this, let it emanate right round the back, passing right over the medulla, and then let your whole head sag. Drop the shoulders and think of the tune, allowing it to really take charge. Then hold your head high and deep breathe the melody into you, sending it round the whole of your head.

The violin has a very soothing effect on some people, but not on others, the piano too. But the harp and flute together, being very redolent of the music of the spheres that emanates on that level, does lift most people in a spiritual sense, helping them to get the bodies into alignment, and a smooth, expansive process established within the system.

And in the morning when you feel you have got out of bed on the wrong side, start the day by humming your favourite musical piece. Feel it bringing you to life and clearing all sluggishness away.

Too many people today are taking too many pills to control the nerves. Tension and fatigue arise out of this. And for this it is good that some stirring martial music be heard or created by the mind. Now, you might think that we would want something soothing for this, a waltz perhaps. Oh yes, but later. For this utter nervous breakdown it is necessary at first to get the martial element into the music so that the will of the patient can be aroused. You know how martial music stirs the blood and makes you feel that you can step out and conquer the world. The will is so necessary, because without this in the patient, the healer can do nothing.

This brings us to the first of the physical conditions, to the souls who unfortunately lose a limb in an accident, or where paralysis comes into their body. Here the soul has a great battle indeed to accept what has happened, that life must be conditioned accordingly. Of course harmony and music must come into the picture, and once again you must begin with the martial music. You see, even though the warlike music has its discords, the wrong elements within it, which lead to such tremendous clashes on your earth, it nevertheless sets up a striving within the blood, a stirring within the nerves, a stirring within the whole system. And nowhere is it more appropriate than when a person feels so depressed, wishing he could leave this life, because his body is no longer a whole body, no longer able to function freely. The martial music helps to get the etheric working unitedly with the physical, making him feel an incoming of the breath of life that is of spirit. This is the only time we would recommend the drumming. In other conditions it would bring in the argumentative, conflicting energies.

With some people on the brink of suicide the only thing to use is 'The Lord's Prayer'. If they cannot accept it, then you will have to work on the invisible vibrations. But do it at the same time each day. The rhythmic process is so necessary. It builds up power for the absent healing to be effective. Miracles can happen. If the healer is persistent, people who are so near suicide will feel a force coming to them that will stop them.

We could tell you tales of many souls who have been knocked down utterly by the loss of limbs, by paralysis, and how they found themselves able to live lives of service in their maimed bodies. They did it because they placed themselves in the way of receiving, which is the only way to accomplish in this life.

Once the patient has got on top of some crippling condition, but while still a little unsteady, then the more soothing music may come in. There can be the trilling up and down the scale, and the colour needed is the African violet. The patient should be encouraged to breathe this shade into his whole being.

We are aware that at present this music and colour healing is very much in its infancy, but those of you who can heal, who are becoming more colour-conscious and more musically minded, will enter much more into this with the patients as time goes on. Breathe in the music and the colour and get the patient to do the same. When you use the martial music, be sure to involve the patient. Get him to think of a tune, Souza's 'The Galloping Major' perhaps. He can hum it, and this will help you heal him.

The metabolic toning up needs the martial also. See it going through the pores, with the orangey-yellow ray. And the martial is needed with anaemia. Here it is necessary to stimulate the corpuscles with the red and white colours. See them going into the blood stream.

For a depleted immune system, as with Aids, and with these depleting viral illnesses such as M.E., stirring quick tempo music is needed and one should bring in the pearl ray as well.

And now on to the many postural diseases. The spine can get out of place. The whole body hangs on the spine, and it is necessary that good carriage is there. Now an important colour for spinal complaints is the Egyptian blue. This should be seen as rays coming through the patient's head. The musical vibration for this is your own tonic solfa. Allow this beautiful blue to come through the crown of the head and right down the spine, intoning the scale, doh, ti, la, soh, fah, mi, re, doh as it descends. With the spine you always start with the high note and go

45

down to the low. It is good as you do it to feel very anchored to the earth. Take that final D sound and allow it to split, going through the legs into the ground. Then you must always bring it up again.

Somebody whose spine has been put out of alignment through physical accident or perhaps too much exertion must always feel that the weight of the body is going down to the toes. He should be encouraged to hold the arms very slack as he slowly raises them and then lowers them back down, ten times once a day at a smooth pace. At the same time think of the musical scale that is coming through the crown of the head to the base of the spine.

With cancerous conditions that build up and which so often need the surgeon's knife, there can come about a clearance, a dispersal with the resulting discharge through the bloodstream and the orifices of the body. But the healer must become finely attuned, must feel this incoming of something alive, something that wants its voice heard, and along with the music will come the colour needed.

For instance, with some forms of cancer there is a very high note that is held onto in the mind which becomes phosphorescent with a very strong reddish-orange light. This, used in conjunction with the dispersing power of the steel ray and with the silvery ray coming into it, will enter in where the cancer is and work to break down the condition.

Always send out the thought to your inner guide for the correct note of colour to emphasise. Complex gradations of colour have to be gone into with some patients, and that is where healers must work a little harder to understand. It is training, much as a doctor would do, to get the knowledge - but you have to do it by going into the quiet and seeking that this may become more manifest within you.

Sometimes kaleidoscopic colours will come into your mind when treating a patient. As you become more colour conscious, so you will find the subtle hues coming forward, and when your intuitive process has been fully awakened you will feel the musical intonation that gives

46

them life. Colours are dead without music. All round your earth the music is penetrating everywhere, especially in the world of nature. If you could listen, you would feel the green of the grass tuning into the music that is helping it to grow.

You know that in the beginning was the word, and it was the word which brought the physical body into manifestation. The creative thought of the creator coming out of the word was set to music. This was the process by which the great creator worked, and the earth and man came into being out of it.

And now on to the locked limbs - the rheumatism, the arthritis, the acidity within the body and the flatulence that gives the digestive organs too much to cope with. We find the middle note is best for these, a middle note that goes right down to the low. And a colour for the release of locked limbs, the orange with a little bit of red coming in. As you get this coming into your mind allow it to stream through your body and out, surrounding the patient completely. It is needed that the auric field shall be revivified so that the nervous impulses can be heightened, awakened and brought more to the surface in the patient and this condition cleared.

With sluggishness of the liver and kidneys use the long vibrating chords as in the music 'Reverie' where the notes lean back and pause before the little trilling notes that run up.

For defective vision, and there are many different eye complaints, we recommend music where you get the notes with bell-like tones, sustained notes, and there are many possible colours depending on the difficulty. For instance, with the blurred vision associated with a liver or kidney condition, bring into those bell-like tones a very soft pearl radiance, the iridescent mother-of-pearl milky pink, and see it surrounding the eyes.

And where there has been trouble which is leading into blindness you could use the beautiful midway note on a harp having within it the yellowy lime-green. See your hands as you put them on the eyes as filled with this colour.

You should have your own collection of music to play when you are healing and preparing to heal. And we do recommend going to a musical concert when you feel the desire to be uplifted. The vitality you receive can be transferred to other people. If you travel home on one of your public conveyances after such a concert, and the tune is running through your head, you leave a vibration in that seat for somebody to enter into. And very often those working in the spirit world will make someone who needs it sit in the seat after you. You leave vibrations behind you wherever you go.

Go forward then with a song in your heart, and a tune on your lips and be a living ambassador for the harmonies of peace.

God bless you all.

PSYCHOLOGICAL HEALING

Everything on your earth has to have a beginning. You cannot see anything that is without a beginning, and yet there is something within man, imperishable, that is the life force of the Godhead that knows no beginning.

We will speak first of that inner citadel, the spirit image of God that is enshrined within man. An image cannot live unless man desires that it should, and there are clear signs today that many have wandered far away from the divine image of the Godhead.

The need to find God is becoming very urgent in your world, which is why you find so much psychosomatic disease and obsessive behaviour in many people who are denying the presence and purpose of the divine in themselves.

We want to help you to see how these malfunctions come into being and how it is possible that, providing there is a true desire aroused within a person suffering from such a disease, he can be helped. Nobody can really be helped unless there is a strong desire to participate. It is true this may be very faint at times with the negative condition holding him securely in its thrall, but as long as the determination is there, then with good will and a co-operative effort between patient and healer, the secure mental health can be restored.

We want to speak of an event that you have recorded in the Bible. When Jesus the great healer released the bad spirits that were possessing a young man those spirits went into a herd of swine, and the herd ran galloping headlong into the sea. What do we see here? We see a man who should have been above his base animal instincts become so allied, so close to the animal kingdom that he began to take on their characteristics. Those possessing entities, which this man allowed to occupy his aura, could not have gone to the herd of swine unless the man had sunk to that level.

Jesus could see that deep down underneath this man was crying out for the god he had allowed to die within himself, and so he fanned the desire into a much greater desire, with the result that these entities went right back into the animals, because their behaviour was on the animal level. The swine perished, it is true, but those possessing entities came through these cleansing, clearing waters lifted up by the power of the Godhead that resided in Jesus and never more did they tread a path of a similar nature. They had been lifted into a new range of experience.

All around us today we see swinish behaviour, showing that many, many souls have lost their footing in a mental sense. And where you strive truly to serve, then some of these souls will be brought to your doorstep to be led by you to a place where the image of God can become alive, informing their night, helping them to greater balance on the emotional plane in order that they may tackle and overcome the obstructions that they are bound to come up against.

It takes a long time for somebody to enter into a mental attitude and atmosphere where he is completely cut off from normal relationships. So let us try to trace some of the steps that link back into past incarnations which have resulted in his having to return with a mind that does not react normally.

Sometimes you see it very markedly in some children who exhibit extremely abnormal behaviour. Now, these children can be helped, they can respond to somebody who is spiritually alive. But this person must realise that the gift of pity, of sympathetic compassion, so closely allied to the divine love of the Godhead, must be poured out and around these little mites.

Unless the healer remains whole within that inner citadel of his being he is not going to be able to overcome the obstacles with which he will be faced. From time to time these little handicapped souls get very out of gear and can make many demands upon the healer, so much so

50

that perhaps the healer feels 'This is too much for me, I can't cope with this' and is inclined to get a little out of temper with them. Now there is a subtle something within that child that will straight away sense this rejection, and he will begin to play up even more.

But when divine love is aroused and is able to register itself on the earthly emotional level then the healer is literally lifting this little soul, so that for a short time it can live, as it were, within the aliveness and the awareness of the healer. And people will often say 'Ah you have such a way of being able to get right into these handicapped children, you seem to be able to arouse something in them.'

Now, even in a handicapped child there is a creativity there, able to pour itself out. With some it may purely be just an ability to perform a little dance. The music should be introduced, so that this child can discover a rhythm within himself and the healer should join in the dance. This will make the child more aware of the rhythmic force that is gathering momentum within him.

Perhaps the child wants colour, would like to paint, and there is nothing that reveals what is going on in a child's mind so much as painting. You should place the colours there and the brush and let the little one with the disturbed mind do what he will with those colours. You let him get it out of his system and onto paper like something being vomited, then study the efforts of the child.

Very often with a mentally handicapped child you find that he wants splashes of fierce reds and rather dull greens and blues. This is because of the repression that he has brought, because of some karmic condition, into this new life. So what the healer should do is question the little one regarding the colours. Oh, it is true the answers won't make a lot of sense, but something within that child has got to tick away because a question has been asked 'why these colours?' And something of what is happening in a karmic sense will arouse itself and make itself felt.

And then the child should be given something to copy, something bright, the orange, the beautiful mauve, mauve particularly, violet perhaps, or purple. Purple is the colour of leadership and you may need some of this yourself. Indeed if at any time you are in some kind of combative situation, you are standing up for what you believe in, for justice, and you feel that someone is getting the better of you, then please put on the purple cloak, the sign of leadership, the sign of accomplishment. It is good to get these little ones working with the powerful colours.

Adult artists too get into depressions because they have not yet learnt to live by the spirit. But they know they can relieve this by painting. It has great therapeutic value. People who have had strokes and who have the urge to paint often find improvement coming in too.

Another thing that can be aroused in some mentally handicapped children is a sense of competition. They may not understand quite why they need to excel, but in games when they have overcome a difficulty, and caught a ball perhaps for the first time, the praise must be forthcoming straight away. They need to be stimulated, and to find within that stimulation that there is a possibility of achieving. This is what they need to know, need to understand, because it lifts them onto a level where the calm peace-giving rays of spirit can come to them.

These little souls are so often lost in a world of bewildering, sometimes grotesque forces. They may be very clairvoyantly alive, may see many of the denizens of the lower spheres. This can be very upsetting for them, causing them to go a little berserk or to beat their head with their hands. When that happens, more particularly with the older ones, your medical authorities place them in a padded room where they are allowed to go on to their heart's content pummelling themselves and banging their heads. But this is no real cure. It just makes them despair because they have been pushed into a place by themselves, surrounded by these denizens of the lower spheres.

The healer must straight away visualise violet lavender colour going straight into the solar plexus of the child, gradually working its way right out, spreading out over the whole aura. And then the warming smile, the beckoning 'Come, come here.' This often takes courage because, when a child is mentally alive with all these disturbing influences, he gets very strong. These entities which are zooming into the loose-knit bodies will pummel anyone who would want to minister to them.

But if you have spent time in contacting that inner citadel you will be able to arouse this spirit of the Godhead and will have no fear. It is fear that makes these entities feel they can make mincemeat of a healer. But where there is absence of fear and a calm control, then they shrink away, they do not like that. It is fear that they feed on, that they live by.

So, let us go on now to these people you meet, very fearful. Some of them dare not leave their homes and go into the street. They have an obsession, they are afraid that some Sword of Damocles may fall on them. How can these obsessions come about? Again we have to look back, because nothing like this can be aroused in a single lifetime. No harsh treatment in childhood can bring about such strong obsessions. Minor obsessions, yes, but not the strong, all-compelling states.

Some people have a mania. Everything has to be just so - perfectly rounded. They will tidy up and re-tidy, keep on at it. Other people must keep washing their hands. What does this portray? It portrays the guilt that has been brought to this earthly life, but it says something far louder too. There must come a time, mostly in adolescence, when a person becomes aware sub-consciously that there are certain karmic events and patterns that have to be faced and straightened out. And until this can be achieved there is going to be an escapism at work and he will not be able to accomplish as he should in this present incarnation.

It can happen that after a time of peace a person suddenly meets up with someone and there is a soul-destroying relationship established between them. Again karma coming up. The soul communication that should have been aroused in each, and a sympathy, with the wiping out of the error that is there, is not achieved. And perhaps they will go their separate ways with each still carrying within a bitterness and frustration.

You see this happening so many times. And usually the one who experiences it, feels deserted by God. You often hear people say 'Oh, there can't be a God,' or 'God cannot be good.' That is because again they are not allowing themselves to enter into any strong, good relationship with a person or with a cause. They have allowed fear to come in and colour, with the consequence that as they grow older so life takes on drab tones and cynicism becomes built into them. Can they be helped? Can they come back?

Sooner or later a person of that nature will find nervous ailments developing and obsessive characteristics, or even something of physical origin. The healer knows he has taken on quite a task with a soul like that, giving extra attention, otherwise that person will not be aroused sufficiently to go through what is required. In addition to laying-on-of-hands healing, the healer must meditate regularly on his patient sending out from the heart centre the white light of purity and he must see it streaming forth to the heart centre of the patient. As it enters and rays up into the head centre, so it must become gold. The whole of the head must be immersed in gold – and the whole of the heart centre in white.

The mind of the healer should be running along these lines 'May the light prevail within this thy child, so that he may be aroused to see himself for the kind of person he is - and may I be strong to bear the hysteria or any disturbances that may result.'

You see, when such a person really breaks down, and it does happen with this technique, then there will be a time of real inner struggle and conflict. The healer will need to give much comfort and support, relying on that strong inward strength, because he will have to remain above all the emotional cafuffle that will be aroused.

Something else we must talk about is the use of music in psychological disorders. Man represses many things within his soul life. He does not like those things to come up into his conscious mind, for he knows that he will feel distress and pain. But if man is going to be an integrated personality then he has got to face up to himself, no matter what things may rise up from the memory.

A great number of people who go over the borderline into insanity have had dreadful things happen to them in their childhood. It may be in the later years, but in most cases it is in the formative years that these things have occurred. They grow up unable to trust people and sooner or later they enter into states of wrong living and distorted thinking and insanity takes over. Now, music can help these souls a great deal.

There are certain types of music that would cause them to break down and weep and this is good - because once they are broken down in themselves they will start to experience that soul sickness which is a belching up of old negative conditions, letting them come right out into the open. And you all know how wonderful it is when you have had ordinary sickness, to get rid of it and to feel once again the soothing influence coming in.

Now the music that we would recommend is for the harp. The harp is, we would say, the purest type of instrument that man can listen to. You remember how in your old testament, during Saul's periods of insanity, David would play the harp soothing his troubled soul. This can work with these mental patients. It is good to start with very gentle sounds. Make the patient listen, cajole him into listening if necessary, and then go on to develop ever louder sounds, right up from the pianissimo.

Sometimes one needs a great deal of patience, and we know that in your mental hospitals this is difficult to achieve. A great pity, because there are so many discordant clashes of hard unruly music in the hospital wards. In the spirit realm when an insane person arrives from your world he is helped back to normality almost straight away, to the degree of evolution and purity that is his.

Some are insane because of the wrongs of the past and they cannot rise out of that insanity as readily as the timid souls who have had to put up with a great deal of harshness around them in their young lives. We find that by reaching these emotionally trapped souls through music, the pure notes of the harmonies of the spheres, we gradually help them get into tune with the life that is theirs in the spirit world.

Very often in your psychological disorders you find there may be two or three spirit entities trying to possess the one on the earth. All sorts of queer ideas come in to this person - and here again music is very helpful. The way to deal with such people is to get them to select music that appeals to them. At first they may choose very foolish things that cannot help them but nevertheless let them have their choice. The idea is to wear them down. Eventually they will say they are fed up with that particular tune, they don't want it any more, and then you can suggest a tune that will help.

They need surrounding. Put them into a visualised bubble, and pour music into that bubble such as your Blue Danube Waltz, (we do like the Strauss waltzes for this work), and let it impinge strongly at the psychic centres (crown of head, third eye, heart, solar plexus, base of spine). Tell the patient to imagine himself in this great bubble filled with the beautiful natural green colour, encourage him to feel the harmonising influences coming to him.

Psychic obsession is perhaps the most difficult condition of all to deal with. Many people get obsessed. There are the drug takers. The mind expanding drugs all too often open the way. Alcoholics, too, and cases where a neurosis has been allowed to gain too great a foothold, or sometimes where there has been a sudden shock to the system which has left a person vulnerable. These people are too psychically alive without the discipline to control it. Their bodies are out of alignment and invading entities get in with too much influence. Often there is a touch of paranoia, a sense of sinister things around. There are the sudden personality changes, and the voices telling them to do things.

Not all compulsions lead to obsession. The do-gooders who interfere because of a desire to put the world to right, speak well from the heart and do not attract the lower elements. No, it is the base things belonging to the instinctual life of the material earth which attract entities who mirror these things.

Of course these people have to be willing to be healed. And as they listen to a tune that you, as healers, have been impressed to tell them about, and begin to arouse their will, so they will gradually find they are able to face the disturbance and ease it away.

But this kind of condition requires dedication on the part of the healer, and a psychic strength to instill the necessary purpose in a patient who is likely to be all over the place with his emotions. Time and time again he will slip back - back into periods of hopelessness and the desire to escape from it. The healer has sometimes to identify with the patient to draw out and help transmute the bad that is there. Things that often are buried deep in the unconscious mind have to become conscious before the patient can become healed.

Before you set out on your path of service make sure that you are relatively free of unresolved conflicts, and have done the necessary training, or you will find yourself embroiled in conditions you cannot handle. So many people are turning to healing in an ego-conscious way. Someone has told them that they have healing hands and they rush out to do it all unprepared and unprotected. It is very foolish.

Everything that you are attracts a response in kind. The ways of darkness are becoming so subtle, and the spiritual aspirant needs to be very careful that there is not some hidden motive behind his desire to serve that will in time reap its harvest in dashed hopes and unfulfilled promise.

Service can be, for some, a way out of facing the self. If you have not gone back from time to time into your own past and relived some painful condition, or discovered with truthful sight your own inadequacies that have perhaps been overlaid by the determination to appear in control of your life, how can you possibly help another soul face up to his inadequacies? A patient instinctively knows whether the healer is able to support him in his dark night of the soul. And some of the deeply based mental conditions that are being faced today require a high order of skill and compassion.

You see, the healer has to develop and refine the healing channel every step of the way. There must be no let-up and no self-delusion coming in. You have taken on a major task for humanity and you must live up to it, to show, through example, that the path of divine service is indeed worth treading.

God bless you all.

RESCUE WORK

It is with great joy in our hearts that we come to talk to you who are willing to come out from the crowd of pleasure-seeking peoples in order that you might serve the world. Indeed it is not just in your little corner of the globe that your services are required. There are many things happening in distant parts of the earth and sometimes you are being used, through your inner consciousness, so that peace or good or blessing can come out of some unsavoury situation there. It is work that must be done with a willingness to give and not count the cost, to fight and not heed the wounds, to toil and not seek for a reward, and only to know in your heart that you are doing the will of God.

We want to stress this will of God, because so often man finds it only through a period of living according to the will of the self. Like the prodigal son he discovers he's living on the husks and the pigfood of life when he might be absorbing of the Rivers of Life through the field of redemption - a path that takes much time and effort to tread.

Banks of the darker power that have been built up in certain periods of the world's history have remained in the atmosphere of the earth to be carried forward by other people using this power to perpetrate their own wrong deeds. Souls on a path of light are now needed to come in and transform these disturbed conditions. This work of rescue needs souls large enough to be channels whereby the power that had been used for bad purposes can now be changed to the good.

There is only one power, that which emanates from God, the good power, the whole power. But man has taken it and used it according to his own purposes and desires. Of course he would not use it thus if he were not heeding the call of the darker forces in operation around him. Some of you who have visited the ancient spiritual sites upon your earth know exactly what we mean, places where, for instance, black mass has been celebrated, or where there has been much fighting and slaughtering of peoples, much pillaging and plundering.

The earth must be treated as a living entity. The earth provides for her children, the sustenance, the air, the ability to grow through the fertility that is her life force. But from past ages the martyrs' blood that has been spilt is still there within this earth and has need of resolution.

When Jesus, the holy lamb of God, was sacrificed as a lamb on the cross of shame, his blood flowed with a redeeming force within it, flowed freely into the earth and mingled with that blood of the martyrs throughout the ages. Blood is the principle of life. The blood must circulate freely through the human frame, must be in a good state, or else the body suffers. In the same way, you have this stream of life with the guiding force of the blood of martyrs resuscitating the blood of those who were perpetrators of evil in so many places upon the earth. It is through the blood that man can rise into a state of redemption.

If you could see behind the scenes how the hierarchical system works you would see there something akin to the circulation of the blood in man's body. And you would see the blood rising up like the sap in the tree needing to receive the greater impulse from the Godhead. These things, of course, lie too far ahead in time for you to envisage, but you would see how man's body is conditioned and is indeed built upon the image of the Godhead.

Now when we speak of rescue service, we would direct you first to where a disaster has happened somewhere. Within a matter of moments there are many people ready to render service - people rushing out of their houses when a train comes off the rails, and so often throughout the wartimes people getting together to do their best to bring something good out of disaster. And very often there are those present who can channel a higher power of upliftment into those situations that can bring release to those who have died so violently.

There are many different kinds of release that we are trying to achieve on our side of the veil. There are the souls who through being weak willed while on earth are hypnotised, drugged, and so fall under the spell of the sorcerers, the wielders of the black power, becoming helpless pawns once they have passed to the spirit world. They move about like zombies with vacant eyes listening only to the voice that tells them do this, do that. And when some fracas is about to be enacted upon the earth the black magician will gather together a whole hoard of his subjects and take them to the place where the crime is to be. There, they will assist along with those elementals also under the magician's control. And then, ranged on the other side, you have the forces of light.

On the earth there will usually be at least one group of people, such as you gathered here tonight, working at a distance on these trouble spots, and those of you with insight, intuition, clairvoyance will register the quiet impulses revealing something of the nature of that being enacted. The source of these events may have lain dormant, through centuries sometimes, imprisoned in the earth, until a clearing, cleansing action can be brought into being, which could also be triggered off when some catastrophe happens in the vicinity. And the rescue group can help in this redemption process.

Now we would say that, of all who have a desire to partake in such work, those of neurotic temperament would be very unwise to do so. The darker forces can get a hold on such people so very easily. No work of this kind should be undertaken without a strong will having first been cultivated.

All channels for light must of necessity be very sensitive souls, but there is strength in sensitivity that is absolutely unknown to those of a neurotic disposition. Even those of you ready to take part in such a difficult ministry must realise that from time to time you are going to feel the burden, just as the Master Jesus did when he had to go away to the hills to pray to get that closer contact with his Father God. So you must meditate and enter regularly into the quiet, to contact that source of power residing within the depths of your being.

There are those younger souls in your midst who are just climbing a little rung of the ladder of evolution. They feel they want to participate, and they should be given the opportunity. Why not? For they also serve who only stand and wait. And waiting is the name of the game for them. They have to be willing to be just the quiet, steady centre, wherein there is an echo of the harmony that belongs to the spirit spheres, and they can be used.

Many who come forward for service will feel nothing, see nothing, hear nothing, and they will wonder whether they are achieving anything. We would say to them, 'So long as your motive is pure, the desire in your heart sincere, there may not be any need for you to register those fluctuations, as some of your brothers and sisters on earth do, the psychic ebb and flow behind the scenes.'

Many get caught up in fanciful imaginings, romancer types, desirous of doing some kind of service in the rescue field, but who have perhaps the picture of themselves as the strong soul charging forth like a knight of old. Alas, these souls come unstuck, for when the heat and burden of it all really comes upon them they can find themselves with an entity from the spirit spheres around them that is most difficult to dislodge.

You see like attracts like, especially in this field, and those who truly want to see the great brotherhood of man getting into its stride, who want to be part of a world that is being released and free, free from the dissension that has ruled man so much through the ages, will be ones to have the patience and the stamina to achieve.

Very often rescue work is needed for souls who have been asleep for a long time, waiting for the trumpet to sound and the graves to give up their dead. And we do really rely on human helpers for this. You see, many people get heavily enmeshed in ideas promulgated upon the earth which make them too earthbound to be easily reached from our side. They need a human transformer through which the truth can flow to them. And so it is needed that the rescuers of earth are taken when in their sleep state to the graveyards where these souls are sleeping awaiting the call of the trumpet, and they are used to channel the thoughts whereby they can be aroused.

Sometimes it happens when there has been some great conflict upon your earth and many have been caught up in it, just as the Jewish people were during the last world war with so many being put to death, there is a crying out for vengeance. The whole atmosphere becomes charged with this great desire for retribution. But should man seek revenge? Certainly not. I will avenge, says God. And so these desires trap the victims in a web of their own making.

Though the mills of God grind slowly, they grind exceeding small. You all know there is a karmic law. Those who commit dire crimes against their fellow man have got to work this out. The mills of God are grinding slowly within their souls. And indeed, long before they arrive at another incarnation, in the spirit world they must needs hear the cries of those that they have put to death. They must feel the agony in their own souls. Whatever you do to anyone on the earth acts like a boomerang, but returning sometimes at a distant point in time. All wrong action must resound within your soul until it can rise up and desire the help of those who are the rescuers, who can come in and show you what must be done for you to be released from the agony - and this is often dependent on the willingness of your victims to forgive.

You can see, surely, a great chord of justice coming through the love of God operating in all spheres of being, and why it is foolish to work against His plan, why you should seek with all your heart and with all your mind and with all your spirit to discover the path, and why you should tread that path well in this your lifetime upon the earth.

Man is inclined to be a lazy, shiftless, selfish being, but in dedicating himself to his fellow man, through his meditations and prayers, he can raise himself up to be filled with a resourcefulness, to have an enrichment that comes only through service willingly entered into.

It is necessary that groups of people such as yourselves should visit spiritual places still in the grip of the past? The earth there has got to receive power that can recharge it. You are all of you centres of power. The bloodstream we mentioned, circulating through the body, keeps the power moving within you - and that power, added to by your spirit inspirers, can, when you are physically present, enter deep down into the earth and bring up from its very bowels all the noxious things that have had life, and in which life still resides.

So each time you go to such a place you are digging a little deeper into the earth. And you are transforming, through your own etheric blood, the soiled blood of the earth into the purified blood which links the whole family of the Godhead in Him.

Sometimes you meet souls who try to dissuade you, who try to put thoughts into your mind, that it is foolish to give your time and energy to those matters when you might be giving them to the making of money and to the pleasures of the earth. They wish to tempt you and if you don't respond they shake their heads and think, 'Here is an idiot.' But never mind. It is better to be thought of in that way than to allow anyone to unsettle or waylay you.

The younger souls in your midst sometimes find it very difficult to come out from the crowd. They give their allegiance for a little while and then they feel the going hard and want to give up. Be specially sympathetic and helpful to these younger ones. And remember they may not wear the young body either. You are all, to a certain extent, your brothers' keeper, and perhaps a word in season to someone today may bring a word in season from someone else when you desperately need it.

You'll find that as this new age comes more into being, those of you who have come in order to discharge a service upon the earth are not going to find the going very easy and there will be a constant need to understand each other better. Very often the powers of darkness get in hoping to break down relationships formed because of service to be rendered to the spirit world. This should be born in mind and great care taken because there is need that the power that emanates from people working in partnership or groups shall remain strong and focused.

Now what happens to those who have trodden the pathway into light a great distance and who have come back to earth to render service, but through their coming disservice is made? The many fallen angels in your midst who have taken on positions of great power over people, where that which should have been pure and good became debased and impure and was used instead to glorify themselves. And so they trod upon the backs of those who dared to get in the way.

These souls leave negative conditions in the atmosphere which are very difficult to clear. And when they pass into the spirit world they have to be content to go to the bottom of the class. All that they had garnered through the ages is stripped from them. They have to work laboriously, painfully climbing the ladder of evolution, thereby releasing the atmosphere that they created upon the earth where, out of the power that was right and good and just, they created many thought forms where the power became perverted.

Everywhere, things must have form. Your thoughts, if you could see them, emanate out into form. But a form with no power in it is like a beautiful statue without life. So the power must be within the form. Now these thought-forms that start out by being very helpful to man, when they become distorted can be used by the powers of darkness to build up vast edifices which have to be assailed by those who have the light in them, and this power transformed.

This is work that can only be done by those who have gone through some initiations of the soul. To be aware of the vast interplay that goes on between your earth and the spirit world would be rather overwhelming for you, but in a small way you can.

You see today works of art that have no beauty in them, yet while they may seem to be without inspiration, they do have a living quality because those who executed them put their own life into them. You see the hideous sculptures where the artists have reflected themselves and related to some of the grotesque and distorted forms that are there invisibly within your universe. These works of art create something in the atmosphere that again is a stumbling block that has to be changed. The forces of light must enter in but only when the artist can see this for himself will he begin to feel a pull to confront these forms that are alive in the atmosphere of earth that have to be redeemed.

In every age God's plan for man is quite different, and for this new age coming in the plan is that the work of redemption enacted throughout the ages must now be brought to a place where one can say 'Ah, now the ground is prepared.' And those who are conscious of this great fact know that as the preparation goes on apace, so there will begin to flow in upon the earth a time of prosperity that is not dependent on your monies or earthly power, or any other things that can resound in the lower earth vibrations. It will come in on the waves of magical power of the Godhead sweeping into the places of preparation and building the conditions that will give man a feeling for the perfect being in the mind of God that he is destined to be.

We know that each one of you in your own particular way has a small feeling for the perfection that is there, like the mustard seed, within. And though you may not quite understand, it is through your willingness to take part, to give of your time, your energy, to respond to those around you from spirit with whom you have agreed to work, and who may prompt you to feel 'Well, I must make a pilgrimage, I must visit a particular place, I must give of myself to this work of rescue.'

You see, the more we can arouse in your soul the desire to live above yourself, above your physical frame, (Brother Ass, as St Francis like to called it), the more effectively you will be able to train it away from the desire for sensual gratification, to make it conscious of the service that it should render to your soul, your spirit, in this your present incarnation.

God bless you all.

66

THE HEALING RITUAL

Many healers engage in a ritual process that they adhere to sometimes quite rigidly and we would like to shed some rays of light on the advisability of this. Man builds power through routine. He goes to work at a fixed time, he eats at set times and he sleeps to a regular pattern and this enables a thought structure to be built up that regulates his life and his progress. It is only when this becomes too rigid that new inspiration cannot find its way in.

Through meditation man is entering into his proper realm. Whether the meditation is an effective one or not does not matter. He is placing his spirit first. He is giving time to release that spirit so that it is going to operate through his heart, his mind, his consciousness. And the earlier in the day a meditation can be performed the better, at a fixed time of course. If one cannot do it early then the best times are around noon when the sun is at its highest point in the heavens, and when you are getting ready for sleep.

In fact a meditation before entering sleep is a very good thing. It clears the mind of the cluttered thoughts of the day and makes you more ready to enter into the things that must come to you when the body is at rest.

Many people find that in meditation their thoughts go haywire. So it might be a good thing to fix the mind on a mantram. There are many mantrams one can use from the very simple to the quite elaborate. But somehow or other the mind still goes racing along on the channels of everyday thought. Now, you should not get exasperated when this happens, but just compose yourself and bring the mind back to the mantram. In time it will begin to gain a natural momentum.

Another thing is a meditation symbol. Symbols are very useful. They do help to focus the mind, and focus is necessary before the whole being can enter into the meditation. The symbol can be a flower, a rose, or a cross of light. It can be anything that you have regard for. A Buddhist, for instance, would perhaps see the Buddha seated in the cross-legged way. Whatever is most suitable for you. But once you decide on a symbol do keep it exactly as it is, so that you can learn to build.

What would you think of a builder who had a pattern for his building and kept changing it, dismantling his structure? He wouldn't get very far, would he? Choose your symbol and stick to it. For those beings in the world of spirit who help with your meditation can use that symbol. They can fill it with power so that it is available to you at times of emergency and stress. You do not know how much help you receive at times from we who serve your world through you. And the more disciplined you are as a channel, the more we can do.

The earth is sick. Jesus Christ and the other great masters laid the foundation for the structure that should be your earth today. They had to absorb into themselves the sickness of the world. They had to change that and allow it to stream from them as healing power. This work is still going on. They made it possible for you who have followed in their path to continue their work, to absorb into you the power that has been misused, that has caused the earth to become diseased, and change it.

As a healer you do this by so identifying yourself with the patient that you absorb some of the badness and allow it to be transformed through you. You offer yourself as a crucible whereby the change can be effected. But only when your mind is disciplined are you ready to be used for this work.

We also wish to speak about the use of various incenses. Now incense does have a powerful effect. It is used in your Catholic churches, the boy swinging the censer with the clouds of smoke billowing forth, you feel the upliftment of heart and mind. You have entered into a different atmosphere where you can become more alive within yourself and a divine healing can take place. You sit in the silence, absorbing that aroma, and all the strain, all the stress just blows away from you.

We would certainly advise every healer to have some incense, not to be used all the time but where there have been very exacting cases and you feel a bit at the end of your tether, not wanting to opt out of the work but just feeling like the labourer who has been stretched to the limit. Sit there quietly and allow the incense to make you into a new being.

Of course you should always start with a prayer before healing, and you should reach out in thought to the patient who is coming. It is good if you can have people there in the sanctuary to support you, who just quietly sit, not healers in their own right, but providing power to help achieve the maximum benefit for the patient. This is their way of service. They should sit with their palms upwards so that the power can flow from them to the healer. When you are developing your own healing gifts the palms should be face down to receive the power.

Everyone has his little ritual. Catholics make the sign of the cross. They are saying to God 'I am placing myself in your presence, and I know I shall be looked after.' We do not despise these rituals, but be careful they do not control you - like the actor who feels he cannot give a good performance without his rabbit's foot in his pocket. Do not criticise anyone for feeling he needs to depend on these things, but try to get him to see that the power must always come primarily from his own channelled resources, with the ritual merely an aid.

Now what about the cleansing of the hands, these purification rituals that many healers go through? We know that some healers are very finicky, feeling that after each patient they must go and wash themselves. This is unnecessary, except perhaps for some who need the symbology in the action to give them or the patient confidence in the early days. But these things should never be rigidly adhered to. As long as you are in a good state, the healing power provides its own cleansing rays, all the time cleansing.

With cancer it is very necessary for the healer to spend a lot of time trying to get at the underlying cause. There may be some deep past grief that has brought into the adult life a sense of futility, perhaps where a parent has died or rejected that one. And this may have resulted in hate being stored up inside that has led to this cancer in later life. You cannot help much until you get at the cause.

Water, when used with awareness, can certainly assist. If the yellow ray is indicated, we would recommend that water be impregnated with this ray. Focus a beam from a coloured lamp into a glass of water or if you have a good imagination see the colour pass from the palm of your hand into the water. Hold it over the glass for at least ten minutes concentrating all the time that the colour is passing into the water. Then give it to the patient to drink.

Now what about candles? Again, a good thing to use. For a long time the candle has been associated with forgiveness of sins, for clearing and cleansing, for the coming to the Father in the churches. And associated with the candle is the need in man to be able to lift himself to the divine through the candle-light.

In the churches people like to light a candle to the memory of someone who has passed to the spirit world. In effect they are lighting a candle in the spirit world to protect and help that person, because some souls have much to come to terms with when they pass. The simple act of lighting the candle with the thought going out means that some power is streaming to the one in need.

Used in your own sanctuary for absent healing, the candle will generate much greater effect when accompanying the power of prayer. And also when you meditate for world peace. Yes, a very good thing.

Some of these more universal rituals have become a source of power through having been added to so often over the ages. The pentagram, the five-pointed star, for instance, is a powerful symbol of protection. Again it is a potent repository of power, but it should only be used in special circumstances, not as a cure-all. It is particularly necessary where you want to help somebody whose personality is being invaded a bit by obsessing entities.

You can add a little mantram said to yourself to accompany the sign of the star: 'I place (and name him) under the protection of Almighty God.' Something like that. And you can place a golden circle around him spiralling it around and around to encase him in a glorious light emanating from the gold. That will give him courage.

There are many occult signs that can be used. The cross of light, for instance. Where someone is ill because of bereavement, see that person and the cross in front of you and say: 'I lift Arthur, who has just lost his wife and is now in a state of depression into this cross of light.' Some of the accumulated power of this sign will then stream to him.

Now, what about the wearing of the white coats? We would always advocate the wearing of white, because this is the purest and most holy of colours. All the colours of the spectrum go into the white and this high spiritual light is added protection for the healer. It gives confidence to the patient, and anything that gives the aura of professionalism should be done - but again, not in a rigid way. Some adults and many young children are frightened by the memory of an unpleasant experience in hospital at the hands of white-coated practitioners. Everything must be adapted to the needs and responses of the patient.

The healing power is a subtle energy which is primarily directed at the etheric form, and some healers are reluctant to touch the physical body too firmly because they want the patient to be attuned to the higher vibrations. But we think that sometimes a bit of firm handling is useful to break up tension in the physical body that is a hindrance to the free flow of the power.

Most patients relate to their condition as being largely physical and so expect to have a physical response. This is why when they feel the rays that bring the sensations of heat and cold with them they are more sure that something good is happening, when of course it makes no difference at all whether anything is felt by the patient. But patients have to be encouraged into a greater belief. They have to be made to understand that most healing does not happen in a moment of time, that there needs to be a slow build-up of good power before physical changes occur. And everything that you can do that leads to confidence coming in that will sustain them through the waiting period can only be of value.

Do not restrict yourself. Open up always to the vastness of possibility, to the many ways and byways of the human condition, and you will become truly a healer of stature.

God bless you all.

THE PATH OF ASPIRATION

It is with that very real desire to reach hearts that we come once again to help you plant your feet a little more firmly along the road of aspiration, that seeks for inspiration, in order that you might become more fulfilled in this your earth journey. Fulfilment means many things to many people. There are those who find their fulfilment by using creative, artistic abilities. There are those who find it in purely mechanical things, who have an inventive flair that can work with the rough materials of earth and produce something useful out of them. And those who love juggling figures, who feel a tremendous satisfaction when raw figures can be turned into a neat solution.

Then there are those who feel that their ultimate fulfilment is in garnering more and more mystical experience. They know the value of meditation, going deeply into the silence where they are lifted into an altitude of spirit that they have not before reached. But they also know that no one gets anywhere without consistent effort upon your earth. In all fields of endeavour a man must strive or he cannot achieve.

Oh, we know there are those parasites in your midst who are always hopeful that they are going to be carried along on a wave of enthusiasm. Sometimes they look as though they are taking part but when the last analysis is reached they must be left behind, because not having made the effort they cannot receive the prize. And life, even here on earth, has many prizes to offer those who are determined to fulfil themselves as far as they can, prizes that accompany the satisfaction of a job well done.

In the new age movement there are many charlatans who latch onto any glamorous road to recognition. One of these is the field of crystal healing. Certainly your precious gems of the earth have a quality of life that has been gathered through vast ages of time and anything that has lasting quality, that becomes more full of life as time proceeds, must of necessity have value for man. But again, this value can only be realised through effort.

If you hold up a crystal and gaze at it, even though you may not have a clairvoyant ability to see within it you can feel the spiritualising energy that will flow right through you, that will open you up to spheres of light. But crystal gazing has been degraded into mere fortune telling, and the pictures that build up within the crystal without a spiritual intent are not images that can bring any sense of a creative ability or a forecasting that concerns itself with the needs and aspirations of a true seeker.

Nevertheless people have continued to wear and covert precious stones, recognising that something of power can flow to them, but the power is weak if the soul receptivity is not there. Some healers wear crystals around their necks when healing, and we recommend this, provided they are gems of quality. A diamond can be very helpful to harness the healing vibrations as they come through. The mineral qualities that have been compressed over vast aeons of time can bring real energy. A gem gives off radiations, and also attracts the sun's rays. The sun shining through it brings out all the many colours, the radiance there, projecting them outwards.

For sufferers from certain blood disorders the pure ruby would be most helpful. Jade brings a firmness of character, a serenity of disposition, and for the healing of the mind it is good for the amethyst to be used. Anyone who wears a piece of pure amethyst while in a depressed state, if they keep touching it, holding it in their hands now and again, would find it helping them to become more in tune, helping them out of their depression. And aquamarine can bring power to remove unwanted things from the body such as foreign objects and toxins.

But the ability to really use these special healing tools is relatively rare, because of the superficiality of approach that so many people bring to them. And there is a price to be paid if these things are misused, because wrong motive can lead to a degradation of the power, and a descent into the realm of illusion.

Life lived in the earthly body is full of unreality. You only have to watch the passage of the days, the months, the years to see how unreal this transient, fleeting mortal side of life is. But that which irradiates and shines through the mortality of life, the immortal part, we would liken to a gem, and the more you care for this gem, this spirit, the more you will be able to feel in your soul life a stirring of the image of God which lies with the spirit. You will enter into a state of timelessness, where the deleterious things of time and sense here on the material plane will not affect you.

There is also a healing power that can flow in because of meditation. The deeper the meditation, the more value it has. Although at the time you may not seem to receive a great deal of enlightenment and there is no sensing of any mystical experience, nevertheless, as the moments go by, thoughts filter into the mind because the will has been stirred to make the effort, enlightened thoughts that can give sense and direction to all that you are preparing to achieve.

Unless a practitioner acknowledges God and is striving to walk in the pathway of light he cannot build up satisfactory communication between the patient and himself, so that the patient can bring himself to reveal that which is working in the depths of his being.

Only fully prepared healers can support a patient in soul crisis. Healers who have faced the dark recesses in their own souls, have learnt to deal with what they find, have experienced the grace of God, have opened up to the understanding souls around them in the spirit world and have gone through their own trials and experiences of the way - only they can say to the patient, 'Trust me, I have been there before you,' and then, with a generosity of heart, identify with the soul of that one, taking on some of the burden.

Such a healer is following in the pathway of the disciples of old, bearing the burdens of the weak. He has the ability to draw on the power of his own experiences and resources to lift himself above the negativity he is faced with.

As we look around we see many centres devoted to healing, we see many people practising healing, but few capable of sustained power. Healers who take on difficult cases find that a transference, a soul identification with the patient occurs. Oh, even the less developed may be able to lead that patient to a point where there is a willingness to get at the cause. But in more capable hands they would both be able to enter into a greater understanding of what had gone wrong, so that there could develop within the patient a more enlightened outlook opening out into a state of health. With an incompletely trained healer the task becomes too much and the negative forces all too often come in. He may get the ill health himself and even become neurotic.

The strong desire to heal, to be the one who succeeds where others have failed, where the ego is strongly involved, or where he believes that unless he can feel keenly the weight, the burden of the sorrows of others within his own being, he is not achieving, all these things keep the healer down on the level of the condition and open him up to repercussions.

All true aspiration is the aspiration of the soul towards service, but we say to every would-be healer who has not yet come through the fiery trials and testing experiences needed, has not gone through the initiation time of rigorous soul training, that you should apprentice yourself to someone who has. You may come into contact with someone in whom the light has vanished, the unhealthy soul, and the sympathy is there, and you feel the stirrings of the need of that one. You may feel that God has sent an opportunity for you to help, but it could be you merely have to pass that one on elsewhere. Maybe this is the first step on the path of the spiritual training necessary in order that the faculty of discrimination and the gift of true compassion can grow within you.

The word 'compassion' is so often associated in the mind with the attitudes and concerns of earth, but this is quite wrong. There is a way of looking at even the worst tragedy that could happen on the earth, to see it as it really is, not as it seems to be. We take the instance of someone being shot out of their earth body very quickly, with perhaps a bloody mess all around. If you had clairvoyant sight you would see the astral body and the soul body rise up out of the shattered earth body and you would see caring spirit-folk around helping this person. Then the transition would not be so keenly felt.

Later when this one must face the karmic circumstances that led up to this violent passing, when he must enter perhaps a little more into the cause of this effect, there something must be unfolded to him, then he is helped up. What to mortal eyes is such a tragedy becomes an opportunity for the spirit beings around to render service to the earth. These ministering souls bring comfort and peace to the loved ones left behind so that they too can register, out of the shock, that the body is only like a coat that is cast off, that there is something more stable and firm within that transcends death. And after the first paroxysm of grief has past they will be able to rest on that firm strength, that stability within themselves.

No sense can be conveyed to the mind without the backing of spirit. And everyone has to go through a chaotic time before he can really enter through understanding into that abiding peace. That is what most people are striving after - a peaceful contentment upon which they can rest. So it is necessary that man should cultivate the right kind of will.

There is self will, there is God-directed Will, and there is a will that holds the balance in between. You see, self will, when put into proper channels, where it becomes a seeking after the true self in order that the God power shall become alive within the soul, that is what we are speaking about as the balance in between.

When one enters fully into the discipline of training thoughts, training feelings, in order that the higher Will may live and bring in the fruits of its cultivation, then real progress is being made on the spiritual pathway. And the ways of healing entered into will have real power backing them, even the miracle-working power.

You know, when Jesus changed that water into wine, the first miracle he ever wrought, he could not have done it without the power of concentrated thought - but thought which had feeling entering into it. A thought without feeling soon becomes dogmatic, capable of inflicting heavy burdens on other people. But of course wrong feelings can come in with the thoughts and can be woven into the texture of the will so that a person becomes a pawn in the hands of the evil-doers on the spirit side of life. This cultivation of too much self-will without being God controlled can very easily hold sway as it has done in many countries on your earth backed by the structures and tyrannies of the darker kind of power.

Very little is recorded of the vast healing ministry that was carried out under the guidance of the master Jesus. You do not hear of the seventy who, though not ready for the more heavily laden work, were sent out by the master to teach and to heal, and who brought those they could not help to the disciples. And Jesus himself at times became worn and spent when he had to heal where the disciples had failed. Oh, the struggles the disciples had with their souls and with each other. You get nothing of this.

You do get how, after they had betrayed their master, when they were together in that very unhappy state, the light that Jesus had in the first place been able to bring through the channel of His being now flowed into them, making of their spirits candles of the Lord, which flamed up in all their glory. And so they were able to function in the divine way of healing. This surely is what every healer should be aspiring to, the divine way of healing.

To draw this lecture series to a close, we wish to show you some of the paths that healing and human endeavour will take in the future, so that your aspirations will fit more precisely the demands of the spirit purpose, so that you will act with that positive will you have been cultivating, with a strong, driving force behind it. Your will must be like steel, of the kind exercised by Jesus and the other great masters, some of whom are with you now, at work, but a will tempered by the compassion of the angels.

You must discard the weak, the negative thoughts, those that say you must fail, and press forward even when in the grip of the fear of failure that resides in the pit of the stomach, that churns you up so. Until you are able to turn this negative power into the positive power of transformation, no crystal, no mantram, no method or belief will bring in any lasting alleviation or comfort.

It is an inner experience that all who aspire to tread the path of divine service must pass through, to really get deep down into the valley of turmoil before you can find yourself good and strong, able to feel and know, and be surefooted on the pathway.

We do envisage that as this Aquarian age comes more into being there will be many new ways of healing that will reflect the fruits of man's endeavours, your endeavours, as you strive to attune your bodies to the music of the spheres.

Some of you who heal disturbed states in the future will have an instrument like a tuning fork that can produce the note necessary to get into the patient's inward being.

Man's body will gradually undergo change. It is already beginning to lose its heaviness. It will be much easier then, with the different atomic structures, to accomplish healing. Man will respond automatically from the freedom he finds within himself, because in getting to know himself in the various departments of his being he will open up to the streams of power from deep inside the earth which will make him a lighter, a more moveable person altogether.

People are going to make their bodies more responsive to the beautiful swirling movements of the dance of the cosmos. Older people will feel more of an aliveness in the limbs, more of a spring in their step. And they will open up to the rays of rejuvenation that can overcome some of the deterioration. They will no longer feel the need to swing backwards and forwards on the poles of time and conflict, but will feel that eternity is already present with them. This will release them from the fear of death. And when the end comes the body will slough itself off without the desperate struggle that now so often accompanies the final sleep.

Much more healing will be done without any physical contact between healer and patient. It will be achieved by astral contact. For instance, a healer may hear of a sick person living in France, and he will pray, enter into the silence, and voluntarily leave his physical body to visit this person via the astral.

Astral travel is to come very much to the fore in the future. There will even be special schools where it is taught. The healer visiting the patient in another country will be quite conscious of doing so, and will arouse something in the depths of that patient which in time will register in his conscious mind.

The miracle-working power will be much more in evidence then. The ability to change water into wine can only be achieved by a master. To a master everything is there, all he has to do is to give the command. In the hands of someone lesser it cannot operate in the same way. With the creator there is a magical quality - we use that word because there is no other to describe what we want to say. But you know the power of magic, how it changes something immediately. You say 'open sesame' or something, and this power of magic steps in. Think of that, and think of the true alignment that a master has, of the mind, the spirit, the soul operating together as a trinity of being so that in a flash he can draw on the magic of the Godhead. This goes beyond the comprehension of you here, but it is true.

Nevertheless, the lesser miracles of healing are open to you. Anyone who is a healer must of necessity be alive with the real quality of life. But it is what you make of that healing quality that decides how you will develop. A special ability can use a person and spoil a person - but if you use the ability and do not let it use you, then you will find the inspiration comes through, making you more

80

aware of the things you must achieve in order that your way becomes a thing of divine transformation and beauty.

Did not one of your poets say that truth is beauty, and beauty truth? Anything that is beautiful and lifts you onto a higher plane has got truth there. No edifice built on lies can endure, nor on half-truths and compromises. But you will find that as you strive to live in your world as you know it today you will be tempted by the ways of materialistic men. The over-charging, the exclusivity, the seeking for acclaim, all these things would keep you below your true ability, and may even cause you to lose your ability altogether. You must realise that there is a freedom of the spirit that can not only help you do good work and achieve your goals but also provide you with all the necessities of comfortable living without the need to compromise your talents.

Very often when you are hard pressed and in a tight corner you cry out in grief to the spirit and help comes. It may come at the last minute. Miracle-working power is not dead. Faith is still a potent force on your earth. And we know that with the sure knowledge garnered through years of preparation you will avoid all the pitfalls that will of necessity come in to tempt and test you - so that you will tread the path of higher service and, through your aspiration, be an inspiration and a guide to many.

We lift into the light these Thy children. May they go forth to shine as stars in the darkness, and may Thy love be with them now and always.

Amen.